MY MOTHER, MY FATHER

MY MOTHER, MY FATHER

On Losing a Parent

EDITED BY
SUSAN
WYNDHAM

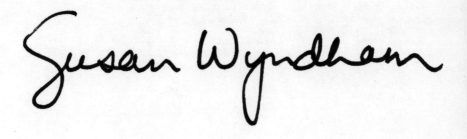

ALLEN&UNWIN
SYDNEY · MELBOURNE · AUCKLAND · LONDON

First published in 2013

Allen & Unwin
83 Alexander Street
Crows Nest NSW 2065
Australia
Phone: (61 2) 8425 0100
Email: info@allenandunwin.com
Web: www.allenandunwin.com

Cataloguing-in-Publication details are available
from the National Library of Australia
www.trove.nla.gov.au
ISBN 978 1 74331 415 9

Internal design by Sandy Cull, gogoGingko
Cover photograph by Sandy Cull, gogoGingko
Set in 13.25/17pt Granjon by Midland Typesetters

Printed and bound in Australia by Griffin Press

10 9 8 7 6 5 4 3 2 1

This project has been assisted by the Australian
Government through the Australia Council, its
arts funding and advisory body.

The paper in this book is FSC® certified.
FSC® promotes environmentally responsible,
socially beneficial and economically viable
management of the world's forests.

CONTENTS

INTRODUCTION

WHEN MY MOTHER DIED IN August 2011, I was caught in such
a violent collision of emotions that I couldn't make any sense
of her death or see that I would ever emerge from the chaos of
grief. Some of my friends suggested I keep a journal about the
experience as a record and a way to seek some understanding,
but for a long time I couldn't even begin to translate my
thoughts into coherent words on a page.

Instead I went looking for writers who had already found
the words for me. A lot has been written about loss and grief,
much of it therapeutic, but what I wanted were personal
stories with which I could identify. Evidence that I was not
alone or mad. I found it in unexpected places; for example,
in an exhibit at Tasmania's Museum of Old and New Art in
which the founder, David Walsh, had written, 'Every day until
her death I believed that my mother wouldn't die that day.
One day I was wrong.'

One of the most helpful things I read was a single sentence

in Anna Funder's non-fiction book *Stasiland*, in which she abandons her research in Berlin when she learns that her mother is dying in Australia. 'After she died, grief came down on me like a cage,' Funder writes. Yes, I thought, that's exactly how I feel, though I had pictured it as a bubble: the physicality of grief that wraps around, presses down, and removes you from everyday life.

Funder goes on: 'It was another eighteen months before I could focus on anything outside an immediate small area of sadness, or could imagine myself into anyone else's life. All up it was nearly three years before I came back to Berlin.'

People often told me it would take six months or a year, or two to overcome the worst of my grief. It seemed odd that there was any sort of formula for my internal meltdown, but I clung to the collective experience with gratitude and hope.

My greatest support came from talking to friends, and sometimes strangers. I quickly learned to recognise the signs of empathy: a collapse of the eyebrows, a direct gaze, frank words of more than perfunctory condolence. They'd been there before me. I have spent many hours exchanging stories with middle-aged children whose mother or father, or both, have died or are nearing death. As a baby boomer it sometimes seems that everyone I know is entering the same bubble or working their way out of it. We are, as one friend put it, members of an adult orphans' club. Everyone's story is different and so much is the same.

The stories in this anthology grew out of those conversations. These fine writers agreed to share their personal memories of loss and grief and recovery because as storytellers they know that death is one of the great universal dramas, and as grieving children they could see how such a collection might help others. Many of them said writing their story was an intensely emotional or cathartic experience. I am touched by their honesty and eloquence, by the clarity with which they observe their own complex feelings, and by the intimate portraits that emerge of their parents and themselves.

The book is a tribute to our mothers and fathers, the people who have known us longest; characters from another era who are as familiar as our own faces and sometimes as unknown as strangers. The stories are about lifelong relationships. A part of us goes with them. The pages throb with love as well as murkier emotions—sorrow, guilt, fear, anger, relief, regret—and a fair leavening of humour and joy.

Most of the deaths are 'ordinary' ones, but our parents depart with courage and spirit. We can't really know what they experience in dying; we can't go with them or pull them back, and that mystery can induce a lingering sense of failure. Some died recently, others years ago, and from these different perspectives the writers chart the survivor's uneven arc of acceptance. Two stories about parents approaching the end of life show how, in different ways, we begin to let them go long before the event.

If life is fair, our parents will die before us. If we are lucky they will die when they are old and we are grown ups. But I learned that knowing, dreading and preparing do not lessen the shock when it happens, no matter how old we are. If we and they are young, the blow can be even harder. No matter how far off our own end might be, it suddenly looms closer.

Our protectors gone, we are confronted by moving to the head of the family and to the front of the queue.

And yet we survive. It has been a ridiculous and comforting revelation for me that the world is full of people without parents who carry on living. With loss there is also growth.

Although this is a collection of memoirs, it indirectly raises questions such as whether a sudden death is preferable to a protracted one; whether it is better to die at home or in hospital; how might we better help our parents—and others— at the end of their life. How will we ourselves face death?

They are hard questions and we do not presume to be experts or exemplars, but we hope to offer some companionship, insight and solace to anyone who is or will be a member of the club.

Susan Wyndham

FOR MY FATHER
(1921–31 DECEMBER 2010)

MARGARET BARBALET

I want to shake the bars of every gate
pull all the locks until they break.
I see you in my head, I hear your voice
its timbre only yours, your words like
no one else; your shoulders bent,
your breath, your bony hands giving
me a glass the way you always did:
all those little things, but you are dead.

How can I have these thoughts all day
the strongest sense of just your shape
your old man's walk, your modest feet
the cap those street boys pitched away
ten years ago in Highbury fields; the new
one worn against the wind in Hebden Bridge
your camera bag, the shutter's click:
I ask again, but you are dead.

I ask myself and ask again how did you
do it: slip away? And did you know
it, sense somehow that this last
day would be the end? The day before
I'd pulled the shutters back 'that much'
you said, to let straight in the summer
light, that apricot for one last time
through oxygen, to you in bed.

In my dream you're quite far gone
asleep or worse, and turned away. I know
you're dying in the dream, you're going
to miss them and I call, *oh, look!* You catch
them then, those cockatoos, all white a-whirl
above our heads and that's the end; except
I learn, some months much later what it
meant: about those birds, about the soul.

---

* *Barkindji belief holds that white
cockatoos take away the soul of the dead.*

WALTZING THE JAGUAR

CAROLINE BAUM

'BABY, WOULD YOU LIKE TO COME TO THE CAR WASH?'

On Sunday mornings my father often invites me to join
him on this errand. I always welcome the interruption to my
homework, thinking we might stop on the way home to buy
some chocolate. We don't do much together except argue and
eat. These we do aggressively and competitively, with my
mother as unwilling spectator.

The car wash is a novelty in my 1960s London childhood.
Another labour-saving device, like the ones my father orders
from mail-order catalogues and the fancier ones he brings back
from business trips to America.

An early adopter, he installed a fax machine at home before
I had seen one anywhere else. Predicted the future would
belong to computers. Bought that rabbit-shaped wine opener
along with other gadgets and gizmos soon abandoned for new
playthings. Ingenious storage solutions, clever cleaning devices.
My favourites: a spoon with a kink in its handle so you could

---

rest it on the lip of a jam jar; a miniature silver golf-club-shaped utensil that cooled tea (of which he drank copious amounts, weak with one slice of lemon)—perfect for an impatient man always in a hurry.

Other families might go to church, but we commune at the car wash, cleansed physically if not spiritually and soothed into a more serene state by the gentle rhythmic vibrations of the machines as we progress along tracks through various stages— rinsing, sudsing, polishing. I laugh without fail when the car is pummelled, rocked slightly from side to side by the initial bursts from the water jets. I like to watch the long fringes of fabric licking at the windscreen and feel the hum through the car door as the hard bristles whirr, buffing the duco. It's like a fairground ride without the fear.

I don't remember us talking during the seven or eight minutes it takes to get through the wash, so perhaps my father is savouring the same sensations. I pretend that the noises the machines make are a terrible storm from which we are protected. We emerge back into daylight, buffed by chamois cloths to a shellac shine, as if we have undergone a ritual of purification, all the tensions that encrust the chassis of our family washed away. When the car is clean, it's possible to believe we can start again.

Some girls dance with their fathers at their wedding, but I did not have that kind of wedding. Instead, I waltzed with my father in the car. A Jaguar, updated with the release of each new model, but always navy with a walnut and maroon leather interior, proof that my father is a self-made success, the deserving owner of a sleek, purring prestige pedigree cat.

We are in France on our annual summer holiday in the south, a pilgrimage to temples of gastronomy carefully chosen from the Michelin guide. Everything about our family is deliberate. My father is a planner. He reads train timetables for relaxation. He is in the travel business so even our holidays feel like work. From a precocious age, I know the differences between a four-star and a three-star hotel, how to assess whether a room is adequate in size and comforts. I make friends with concierges and am an enthusiastic patron of room service. My collection of hotel miniature soaps, shampoos and unguents is second only to my collection of shells.

I am five, maybe six years old. My father sits me in his lap, puts my hands on the black ridged wheel of the Jaguar, and leads me in swooping zigzags along the cypress-lined roads of Provence in dappled sunlight, following the shimmering, swirling cadences of Strauss and other Viennese compatriots of his own childhood on an eight-track stereo cassette (the latest innovation in sound technology).

He is never playful or light-hearted except in that moment. An uncharacteristically spontaneous and carefree episode in a life that was always disciplined, timed down to the last minute and strict in its formality: I was expected to curtsey to visitors. His wardrobe said it all: racks and racks of meticulously hung silk ties, bought in Paris, organised by colour. It was my job on school days to select one to match his handmade shirts and accessorise my choice with a silk handkerchief from a glass-fronted drawer. I loved to run my hand through the weight of their heavy tongues, feeling their dense opulence.

But I feared my father, even when he was in a good mood. His hugs were too tight and nearly suffocated me. His pale British pork-sausage fingers held my hand to cross the road in a vice-like grip. His footsteps shook the landing of the upper floor of our house, his snores rattled doors. It was like sharing the house with a giant. On Sundays he would play recordings of classical music at deafening volume, conducting at his own tempi, bending my mother's knitting needles with the force of his strokes.

On departure days before just about every holiday he would erupt in a sudden temper tantrum, turning purple with apoplectic rage, slamming doors, swearing at the top of his lungs, causing my mother to barricade herself in her room until the moment it was time to head for the airport, usually in tears.

When I was disobedient or exposed in some petty lie, he beat me with a leather travelling slipper. It was as humiliating as it was painful, more so because he'd insist that after the punishment was over, I give him a kiss on the cheek.

By my teens we were openly at war and I wished he would die, leaving my mother and me alone. We were both marathon champions at feuding. He would simply refuse to speak to me for weeks at a time when I had displeased him, ignoring my presence at the dinner table, which, when there are only three of you, makes for a very tense atmosphere. I could match him sulk for sulk, leaving my mother exasperated between us, unable to broker peace, lacking the confidence to intervene and troubled by her own memories of a brutalised childhood.

Conflict was our default setting and it became so familiar as to be almost comfortable.

There were rare moments of harmony. Most of them in the Jag, as my father called it—surprisingly, as he was not usually one for nicknames and rarely succumbed to verbal laziness. As a child refugee, he took great pride in mastering English till he spoke it better than most natives with a posh accent. Together with the car it made him seem like a Tory when he was in fact a passionate Labour voter.

He drove me to school every morning for twelve years, the car foggy with the haze of his chain smoking (Benson & Hedges Special Filter, my job to push the lighter in for him. Then, oh horror, I deliberately inhaled that delicious first hit of burning tobacco, which blended perfectly with the slightly faecal sweet smell of the car's leather upholstery).

In the Jag he treated me more like an adult, discussing world affairs, explaining the history of territorial disputes in the Middle East or old enmities between European nations, his grasp of history dazzling in his ability to quote from speeches, to string together dates into chains of events across centuries, to draw maps of changing and disputed borders in the air, while displaying his natural aggression as a driver, a split-second-reflex overtaker, tailgater and lane changer, intimidating other drivers with showy manoeuvres.

His driving made me feel ashamed. On the passenger side I often met the irritated or more openly angry gaze of drivers he had cut in on. Sometimes I could see their lips move as they swore at him. At times I would adopt a sorrowful pleading expression as if I were his captive begging to be rescued, but no one volunteered.

My mother was his most anxious passenger, sucking in her breath loudly and wincing when he almost grazed other vehicles. On these occasions, when he was showing off or conducting a silent row with us, I met his aggression with feigned indifference, refusing to give him the satisfaction of a reaction while my mother gripped the seatbelt with white knuckles.

But sometimes we shared the road peacefully. When I was seventeen and at summer school at a US college, we drove together from Pennsylvania to New York, finding a sustained serenity in the rhythms of Route 209 until we were stopped by a police motorcyclist and my father was fined on the spot for speeding.

'Don't tell your mother,' he said, establishing a complicity between us that endured through years of such episodes. I never betrayed him and was soon losing points on my own licence, having inherited his lead foot.

He taught me how to park in the tightest spots, reversing into position with one elegant manoeuvre ('Never buy a car without power steering,' he advised, giving the car credit for his skill), leaving a hair's breadth between the Jag and other cars, as the French do.

When he needed to park in the centre of London he would pull in to the forecourt of a hotel where he knew the doorman, hand over a fiver and say in a genial and offhand way, 'Look after that for me, will you?' before we walked through Knightsbridge, Soho or Piccadilly on some retail errand. My mother found this embarrassingly ostentatious but I liked the efficient and lordly way he could dispose of the car without having to endure the endless circling for a meter that would run out before we had achieved our goal.

'Papa, what's that funny car with the bashed-in roof?' I point to a red Mercedes 280 SL. I am ten years old and the concave curve of the roof, together with the car's sleek elegance, catch my eye.

'When I grow up I am going to buy one of those,' I announce with the kind of aspirational confidence my father encourages.

'Over my dead body,' my father retorts.

'Why?'

'Because it's German.'

'So?'

I know the answer already but like to bait my father, enjoying the ensuing argument like sport.

It always boils down to the war. That is why I am not allowed to buy German pencils for school and my mother does not have any German equipment in the kitchen. And yet, my father is a mass of contradictions: he worships Karajan conducting Wagner, even taking us on a holiday pilgrimage to the holiest of holies, Bayreuth, to experience that most Germanic and Hitler-approved cultural festival.

I taunt my father throughout my adolescence with these inconsistencies, but he shrugs them off. He makes the rules, he earns the money, that's that.

'But when I am older I can do what I like,' I needle.

'You can,' acknowledges my father, nodding with equable reason before delivering his ultimatum, 'but if you do that I will disinherit you.'

He delivers the half-joke, half-threat punchline with a satisfied smile, which implies he has amassed enough wealth for this to be a significant counter-move.

Fourteen years later I tell my parents I am moving to Australia with my future husband.

My father's despair is limitless. He mourns as if his only child has been struck by a terminal illness. He begs, he cries, he pleads.

He has escaped the Holocaust. He has survived a fraudulent theft that left his business on the verge of ruin and rebuilt it. But this decision breaks him.

'Baby, if you stay, I will buy you a Mercedes 280 SL.'

The pathos of the bribe's appeal makes me blush on his behalf even as I write this.

Easter, four years ago.

My father comes home after a successful operation for bowel cancer. We attribute his disorientation to the after-effects of the general anaesthetic, as the hospital staff do. In the taxi home, his eyes are dull, like those of a cooked fish. When Felix, the concierge, welcomes him home, he says thank you without looking at who is addressing him, as if on automatic pilot, simply parroting a phrase he has been taught.

He does not seem to register that I have come from Australia to look after him, does not ask how long I am staying. It's as if I have always been there or am not there at all.

He goes straight to bed. Later, he has a little supper, and says he needs to go to the barber and will drive there the next day.

My mother and I raise our eyebrows in alarm.

'Remember, the doctor said no driving and no going up stairs for six weeks,' my mother reminds him. 'Caroline can take you.'

'She can't drive my car,' he replies firmly. He has never let me drive the Jaguar. Now it seems the same rule applies to his new car.

The Prius is just eight weeks old. After a lifetime of loyalty to the same iconic brand, my father swapped the status of gas-guzzling luxury with enviable grunt for sedate green-cred, largely at my urging. I was surprised at this sudden recognition that perhaps a fast, expensive car no longer suited his retired, more modest circumstances. He talked about the Jag with sentimental regret, as if reminiscing about a cherished departed friend.

'Of course she can. You put her name on the insurance papers, didn't you?'

'I don't remember.'

We leave it there.

At two in the morning I am woken by a shuffling sound; it is as if a large furry animal is snuffling through undergrowth. Still disoriented by jet lag, I think it's a wombat outside a tent, before recognising the sound of my father's tread in his leather slippers, then a jiggling of keys, the zipping of a bag, the fumbling for the front door chain and bolt, the turning of a handle, the soft clunk of the door closing.

Where on earth could my father be going at this hour? I rummage for clothes, call the security guard downstairs and tell him to stop my father at the gate if at all possible. He says my father has already left the building.

When I get outside it is snowing, the loose, feathery kind of flakes that fall messily, as if someone in the sky has burst a doona. My father is standing by the car, fumbling for his keys in the darkness.

'Where are you going?'

'To the bank.'

'But it's two o'clock in the morning, the bank is closed.'

'I have to get to the bank urgently.'

'But it's dark, and it's snowing, and the bank is closed. Why don't we go inside, have a cup of tea and I'll drive you there when it's light? You remember you are not allowed to drive?' I say, reaching coaxingly for his arm. He brushes me away, raising what I can now see is his cane, as if defending himself from an attacker. There is a wild look in his eye, like that of a horse when it shows too much white and is about to kick.

It takes me forty minutes to persuade him to come back inside. He seems oblivious to the cold although he is only wearing pyjamas and a light dressing gown. He does not shiver, whereas I cannot stop my teeth from chattering. I make us both tea, lead my father by the hand back to bed (he has slept apart from my mother for years, snoring being the official excuse for a much deeper estrangement), lock the door and hide his keys.

In the morning it's as if the episode never happened. My father seems more alert and lucid, scans the newspaper, seems able to focus on his breakfast and announces that he will go

16

to the barber. I remind him that he can't drive and offer to take him.

'It would be better if I drove,' he insists.

Once he is dressed we go downstairs. When we reach the car he says, 'I cannot let you drive.'

It takes half an hour to persuade him to get into the passenger seat. Once there, he settles down, gives clear, precise directions, knows where to find free parking.

'How do you like the new car?' he asks genially, back to his old self.

We discuss its silence and other special merits in the way of trainspotters or bird fanciers.

We walk to the barber, my father's brisk step and unfailing sense of direction intact.

I am the only woman there. The barber, a young Lebanese man in his thirties, greets my father, a regular customer, with courtly reverence as he goes about his lathering and shaving with a blade. I savour the atmosphere of testosterone, as generations come and go to be trimmed and clipped. My father smiles benignly into the mirror, surrendering to the trusted ministrations like a grandee favouring a servant. It must feel good to have the bristles he grew in hospital disappear, to have hot towels applied, to feel the caress of the badger-hair shaving brush and the precision of the razor expertly handled.

I think of the car wash, of these rare moments of peace that we have shared, of how cleaning is common to them. When I was a little girl and had inherited his habit of biting my nails to the quick, he used to soak my hands on Sunday mornings in soapy hot water before inspecting each finger individually, admonishing me and then slathering them with hand cream. It was probably the most peculiar ritual of our relationship and never cured me of the habit.

When my father is done, the barber helps him on with his coat. His dignity and fastidious care about his appearance have been restored, and with them a new vigour has returned, a slightly sprightlier step, a shinier eye. My father seems able to take in more of his surroundings with each passing hour; I can sense his condition improving as if mist is lifting from a landscape.

'Let's go next door, I want to show you their pastries,' says my father in the conspiratorial tone of my childhood when we would egg each other on in exploits of gluttony—I rarely won the contest of who could eat the most mountains in a block of Toblerone.

We buy meringues that look like the Alps and Florentines the size of small pizzas. The outing is a success. He does not argue about who is driving when we reach the car, compliments me on retracting the car mirrors (one of those typical extras he loves to indulge in) to handle a narrow stretch of road.

My mother is so delighted she opens a half-bottle of champagne and we all toast my father's recovery, he with a sip, we with the rest. He eats lunch and for the first time since my arrival, my mother laughs and pinches his arm affectionately, pleased to have him back.

Afterwards he goes to bed for a nap. As I tuck him in, he smiles up at me, his face lopsided and crooked. It reminds me of a photograph I have of him before he left Vienna in 1938. He must've been nine years old. The smile he gives the photographer is a mixture of charm and shyness. I see this on my father's face for a fleeting moment and then it is gone. And with it, so is my father. He will never utter a lucid sentence again.

'We have to sell the car,' says my mother.

We are on the number 19 bus riding home from the hospital where she has just been given the diagnosis that makes sense of the previous week's nightmare.

My father has vascular dementia. There is no cure.

We do not know how we will care for him or where. Desperate for certainty, my mother finds only one: he will not be driving again.

My parents never had a wide circle of friends; the few they were close to have mostly died. They do not socialise or entertain and retirement has not brought new people into their lives. Now what remains is a handful of my father's former colleagues and business associates. Their Christmas card list has diminished to a dozen, including Nomi, the tall Japanese owner of a prestige car showroom where my father has been a client for more than twenty years. He has sold my father each of his recent Jaguars, and now the Prius.

At home the air is leaden. Unable to focus on any useful task, I thumb through the latest edition of my father's innovation catalogue, noticing that he has marked up an invention preventing speed cameras from photographing your number plate. Incorrigible, even at eighty.

There are other people my mother could call first—one surviving member of her family, a woman friend she rarely sees but speaks to every week—but instead she calls Nomi. He agrees to take the car back.

After I have organised my father's care, I am not prepared for the wash of anger that pushes me under like a rogue wave out of nowhere. It is so completely unexpected, unpredictable and violent that it frightens me in its opportunistic, random attacks. I did not love my father with this kind of ferocity, so why am I lashing out so fiercely?

I call a part-time counsellor friend for advice. Grief is not her field, and she has limited time, but offers to listen if I can meet her outside her workplace.

A cafe is not private enough. 'Perhaps we could talk in the car?' she suggests.

The very space that defined so much of how my father and I related: it feels right, familiar, safe. There is comfort, too, in sitting facing forward, not having to make eye contact, but it's intimate enough to feel confessional.

Soon I am sobbing, sitting at the wheel, nose running, choking and spluttering fury. Oncoming twilight conceals my distress from passers-by.

After an hour of listening, my friend hugs me across the handbrake and I drive home, exhausted by my outburst, but also calmer, like a volcano reverting to dormancy after an eruption. The muscle memory of each gesture, braking, accelerating, indicating, offers some consolation with its mechanical repetition and achievable mastery.

I wonder if my father's muscles, atrophied as they now are, retain any patterns of the gestures of steering or changing gear now that everything else in his brain is bombed, blasted, derailed. I replay in my mind, over and over, like picking at a scab, our last drive together, the utter banality of it, the lack of portent or significance in our mundane exchanges.

If I had known we would never be able to have a normal conversation again, what would I have said?

When my father is diagnosed, my mother comes to a grinding halt. Like a car with a flat battery she simply refuses to start. Shock has stalled her engine. Her body smells sour: I recognise fear wafting from room to room with her like the smell of curdled yoghurt.

My father paces the ward, shouting for his briefcase. Having tormented the nurses with Chinese rope burns, he calls at midnight, shrill with distress, demanding his passport and car keys. He gets into bed with strangers, steals items from bedside cabinets, disrupts meal times, chews his bedding, tears up the newspaper, makes lewd suggestions to orderlies and escapes with an unsuspecting group of visitors. The police are called to find him.

Psychiatrists interview my father to assess the severity of his condition and determine where he should be placed. My mother and I are invited to be present. To their questions about where he lives and his interests, he delivers an uninterrupted monologue about the build-up of traffic in the neighbourhood, detailing his frustrations with lights that have no right-turn filter, causing crossroads to clog up. Cars, too many cars, fill his consciousness, together with battles with the council over parking restrictions, one-way streets, speed bumps and the absence of zebra crossings. He responds as someone literally driven mad.

Weeks after my father is institutionalised my body is traversed with aches. They begin at my ankles, travel up my legs to my buttocks and into my neck and shoulders, moving like a weather pattern from site to site, waking me at night like storms. The pain becomes more and more acute, combined with a deadening fatigue that leaves me breathless and bedridden for days. I feel as if I have battery acid in my veins.

'If I did not know better, I would think you were poisoning me,' I tell my husband. Blood tests and X-rays reveal nothing.

The pain is corrosive. I give up exercising because it makes me feel worse. I lose three or four days of the week lying prostrate, dozing. I have occasional good days when my energy returns, but the pain always comes back like a punishment, as if my body were saying, 'How dare you think you could cheat me?' Eventually a doctor agrees with my internet diagnosis of chronic fatigue combined with chronic pain—something called fibromyalgia.

'It's a dustbin diagnosis,' he says breezily, 'which means we just chuck all the symptoms into a bin that we can't explain and give it that name.'

The illness affects me for two years.

Then one day, I realise I have had five, maybe six days in a row symptom-free. I feel stronger, have more stamina, the pain is less sharp, less persistent, less frequent. I start making bolder plans, attempting half days and then full days in the city, reclaiming parts of my life.

I've spent the day in Sydney, back in the saddle professionally, attending meetings, going to interviews. No ambushing by a sudden rush of tears, no power surges of rage. A day of smooth, unremarkable transitions.

I drive home feeling elated: my life is back in gear.

I can't wait to tell my husband how well the day has gone, how promising some conversations have been about potential work.

I park at the top of our driveway. Those last few metres always give me a sense of satisfaction, as if I were scaling a small mountain instead of just revving the engine to get up a very steep incline. Through the drawn curtains I can see David's silhouette on the sofa, about to watch the seven o'clock news, which marks a sort of unofficial cut-off point for our working day. I know the wine is already opened. I have a small window in which to debrief him before the headlines begin. I hurry inside.

As I begin my account of the day both of us become aware of an unfamiliar sound, just on the other side of the curtains. Something scraping, with the rhythm of a ricochet, like a tin can being kicked repeatedly along a wall. Metal, tearing. Puzzled, we draw the curtains back.

Where we should see the bonnet of the car, there is a void.

A void.

Where the car—

We run outside. The car is at the bottom of the driveway at

a peculiar angle, jackknifed against a concrete retaining wall. It has come to an abrupt halt, the wing mirrors tearing away fence posts on the descent. The undercarriage has fallen out like the spilled guts of roadkill.

Neighbours, brought out by the noise, look on in disbelief as we hug and do a little dance, punching the air and laughing. The enormity of what could have happened makes us both lightheaded with relief. The car has not rolled down onto the main road or gathered speed and propelled itself across the street into another house. It could have been much, much worse.

When I tell friends what happened, they nod wisely. Clearly, according to them, the episode demonstrates that I am still in shock, still dealing with the aftermath of my father's decline. For months, I buy that interpretation. I am not myself, not ready to venture into the outside world, not self-possessed enough to regain control.

But today I am not so sure. Couldn't it just be that in an absent-minded moment of eagerness to share the news of my successful day, I had forgotten one small gesture of precaution and left the handbrake off? Just how symptomatic and symbolic was that one error?

What would my father have said? Sometimes he overreacted with stinging criticism and sometimes he'd surprise me with a philosophical shrug. I can hear him making a joke of it: 'At least it was only a Holden, not a Mercedes 280 SL, baby.'

I delay taking the Prius back to Nomi until the day before my own departure, dreading the burial-like finality of it. I tell myself it is just another chore on a to-do list that never seems to get any shorter, no matter how many items I tick off.

When it can be put off no longer, I empty the car of the last evidence of my father's ownership and disconnect the GPS he argued with so vehemently, shouting at its implacably calm voice to 'shut up, you silly cow' whenever she urged him to 'make a U-turn where possible' after he disregarded her instructions.

Unplugging that cable feels like switching off life support.

I drive to the showroom in Chiswick, taking back roads, lingering behind the wheel, wondering how often my father used the special feature that warmed the driver's seat on winter mornings and that I now switch on for myself, to give me that cosy electric-blanket feeling of comfort. But nothing can stop me shivering as I approach my destination.

I ask for Nomi at reception. Before I know it, a tall man is standing behind me, all stillness and solemnity. He bows. There is an awkward moment before I stretch out my hand for him to shake. He takes it with his head still lowered.

'We have not met before, but of course I know all about you,' Nomi says, showing me to his desk.

'The Mercedes 280 SL, still your favourite car, yes?' he asks, attempting to lighten the mood.

'The Prius was your idea, yes? Very good choice. Your father, he like this car more than he expect after Jaguar, no?'

Choking, I can only nod.

'Perhaps he will make good recovery?'

I shake my head.

'I am very sorry,' he says, presenting me with papers to sign.

I cannot see them clearly. My eyes swim with tears, spilling down onto forms about vehicle registration.

I rest my forehead on the cool clean glass surface of the desk.

'Perhaps some tea?' asks Nomi.

I brush the tears away, shake my head in a silent 'no thank you', sign the forms and leave as quickly as I can, stumbling between new cars to the bus stop. I get on the first bus that comes, knowing it is the wrong bus, not caring, just wanting to be taken away from that place as quickly as possible.

Such a mundane chore.

It is one of the saddest days of my life.

When I was a little girl I had a plastic steering wheel that attached to the wall by suction. I think about whether a driving toy might help my father regain some fragment of identity, but his carers tell me no. He would only chew on such a thing and hurt his already fragile teeth. On days when we bring him down to the visitors' lounge for tea or when he is calm enough to go on an outing, he gazes at passing traffic with more animation than usual. I watch for a flicker of recognition when a Jaguar goes by, but there is none.

INDEPENDENCE DAYS

THOMAS KENEALLY

THIS IS IN MANY WAYS an infantile piece. Infantilism is in part the condition of children of any age towards their parents. It is inherent in that dreaded cry of so many mothers, 'Remember, you'll always be my little boy/girl.' It's the sort of thing that ensures you can't even attempt to sort out the whole parent–child business without sounding a bit cracked. You can't untangle the ganglia of love, tears, reproach, joy, failed expiation, grief and dense history that connect even the aged living to their lost parents. But you can't stop trying either.

To begin with the mother. A few years ago, I was in transit to Europe by way of Bangkok. We disembarked from the plane by stairs into the stew of the tropic night, and so into buses which would take us to the terminal. I found a seat in the bus but then noticed a woman about fifty years of age standing in the central well. I was about to offer her my seat when I realised that I was perhaps a quarter of a century older than her. It was at that second I realised my mother was dead, and that the voice I had responded to in nearly giving up my seat was hers, and that in fact that voice was not dead, and would not die until I did.

There was a debate when I was young about whether sex or survival was the major driver of human motivation. But for me there is no doubt that, unless there has been total alienation between parent and child and not even then, pleasing one's parents is an intense motivation. Some are also driven to please God or the gods, but that's no different: parents are gods. A mother *is* the goddess, even if her name is Elsie, the name my mother never forgave her engine-driving father for giving her. Elsie or Denise or Judy, the mother is the person who, above all, gives unity to our childhoods. And since in her presence we never cease to be her child, she never ceases to seem more eternal and fixed than the stars. She never ceases to be a given of the universe we inhabit. They'll never make a bullet to get her, any more than they could make a bullet to get Aphrodite or Minerva.

That's why her death is so astounding. She has been our chief praiser and, indeed, our chief appraiser. How are we to survive in the universe without her approval, which has remained, since we were weaned, the spiritual milk which underwrites who we are? She has given us our civic morality: 'Give your seat to the nice lady!' And she beamed when we did. She gleamed when we showed her we were amenable to civic and humane values.

So, after the death of parents, but particularly of the mother, we are left asking what we will do, in a barren universe, to earn merit. The mother's praise is of at least the same, if not greater weight, as the world's. The impulse to earn it is innate. We all make up reasons, and tell stories, funny, confessional, self-effacing, wistful and sometimes bitter, about why each of us is specifically driven and marked by that objective. And forgive me, I am going to join the storytellers' club, since telling the same story differently is in part what this book is concerned with. In this narrative, I'll either demonstrate universal truths or confess to raging neurosis, or both at once.

Let me go further into this well of truth or neurosis by including the father—in my case, Tom, of whom more later. There have been many novels generated by the aspirations operating between father and son. The son wants his father to declare him a friend, a creature of equal valour. That's why they go fishing together or to sporting events: to encounter each other in the presence of champions, and to absorb as equals the gallantry of opening batsmen. It doesn't make a difference if the father is a quivering mass of self-doubt. Because to the child the father has no symptoms. His purposes and manifestations are as mysterious as those of a Greek or Hindu deity. Whatever the effect on us, they all mean something transcendent. And to be included in any of his impulses of kindness or enthusiasm is a sublime privilege.

For a boy I don't think the father business is quite as complex a relationship as that with the mother, the very first of women. But it is true, too, that for a boy the desire for fatherly praise is twinned with a guilty desire to compete, to outclass, to transcend, to become ultimately the father's father, to wring that form of admiration from the old man.

Perhaps I should now slink away and see a psychiatrist. But instead I'll continue.

Since in old age our greatest strengths become what kills us, both my parents died of the same lethal strength and the same disease, their independence.

Tom was a universally loved eccentric and tough guy who believed in *self*-cure, not in a New Age, positive-thinking sort of way, but in a bush endurance manner. He believed the greatest problem with consulting a doctor was the risk of being thought a hypochondriac. If you got sick, you kept still and let the thing cure itself. I remember his saying when I was a kid that vitamins were a fad. 'I knew these old timber-getters in the Macleay and they got by without bloody vitamins.' One other of his aphorisms: 'A man goes into the doctor healthy and comes out with three diseases.' During World War II, when he and other Australians were being shunted around the Middle East and North Africa, they had always been afforded the luxury—by the standards of the Depression—of as many boxes of tailor-made cigarettes as they wanted. My father became a smoker and reverted in his later civilian life to more economic roll-your-owns. At the age of sixty-five he suffered chest pain and waited through an Easter weekend, from Thursday until Tuesday, to get it seen to. As it turned out, it was the smoker's painful warning, a heart attack.

He was treated, went cold turkey on tobacco, walked everywhere—mind you, he and my mother didn't own a car until they were in their fifties—had no further check-ups, and so cured himself. Following his self-help philosophy, when a young Rugby League player in the early 1930s, he had kept a broken collarbone secret until it more or less knit. And likewise when in his late eighties he broke a hip, he asked to be helped to a chair so that he could allow the same knitting process to occur. Such was his horror of medical care! He had sacrificed himself to make my scholarship-boy brother Johnny a doctor, but Johnny worked with children and was exempt from his usual assessment of many doctors, which was that they didn't know shit from clay. The many modern tests they imposed on him in his late eighties and early nineties were nothing better than make-work. Doctors had nothing better to do than frig around with a man.

He hated passing hospitals in a car. He had names for the hospitals he spent time in—for example, when his hip *failed* to knit. The Lady Davidson orthopaedic hospital was named 'Changi'. Concord Repatriation was 'the Death Camp'. Mona Vale hospital, where he died, had long been referred to as 'the Murder Factory'. When he lost his independence and began to fail he saw himself as hostage to a Kafkaesque medical machine.

Although he came of Labor Party origins, he preferred to remain independent of the state, too, and certainly independent of all charity. He applied for a war pension only when a relative who had served less time overseas than he had got one. He was given a book of cab vouchers to get him to medical appointments, but to him a cab was something you caught only to emergencies, or to weddings, and to meet relatives arriving at the railway with plentiful luggage.

This passion to be free-standing, shared equally by my mother, precluded my parents ever buying into a retirement village. After my father's death, my mother still maintained her independence, gently and stubbornly rebuffing all suggestions and brochures and reflections about how the other women in a retirement village would be such good company for her. At the age of ninety-four, having had minor surgery for skin cancers, she persuaded the doctors and nurses that we were collecting her a day prior to the agreed discharge date. We had no choice but to take her home earlier than expected. We insisted that she stay overnight with us, but she refused. In the middle of that night, she fell and fractured her pelvis. She had an alarm button, but had left it by her bed, out of reach. When we found her in the morning and called an ambulance, she maintained that it wasn't necessary, and the ambulances had more severe cases to attend to.

I know that millions of children have similar stories, but again I have ever since these events been fascinated by the fact that the virtues that brought them through the Depression and a world war, that sustained them in less than fulfilling Menzies-era jobs, and that imbued my brother and me with some sense of a future, were precisely what killed them in the end. That our virtues could be lethal had never occurred to me before.

There is an example of dangerous virtue in my father's case. On the last day of his life, I gave him some water, and a few drops fell on his pyjamas. He had always been a natty dresser. Though largely incoherent from dosages of morphine, he was insistent that I change his shirt. There was a fresh one in the cupboard, but since he was so weak it was a struggle to get it on him, and it took a great deal of his strength—I hesitate out of guilt to call it his final reserves of strength. When I had changed the shirt he was satisfied and lay back. He died that evening in the fresh shirt. I know by instinct now that he had changed because he thought he was dressing for work. That was another overriding virtue—industry, punctual performance. In its name, he used up all the hardihood that remained to him that afternoon.

My connection with my father had always been one of unstated love, and I hasten to admit that, for my generation, the fact does not make us exceptional. But in the spirit of such relationships, obvious grief could go unstated too. I remember a day in Penrith early in the war when uncles who were old diggers discussed places like Amiens or Damascus, and my father, himself about to be sent away, joked with them. That day I did something, I forget what, that merited a mild slap from him in an age when resounding slaps were more the fashion. In my five-year-old passion I said, 'I hope the Germans *do* shoot you.' I can barely remember this incident, probably soon forgotten by him, without tears. I was only a child, yet the utterance seems to encapsulate everything painful and double-bladed and unresolved about fathers and sons.

The death of my father in the end was something that seemed to shatter the interior of the earth I stood on. I know it is the same for others, particularly in those old-fashioned, undemonstrative, don't-kiss-a-boy-once-he's-an-adolescent days. So when he went the loss proved so profound that I did not have the instruments on the surface to measure its impact. I wept at the graveside when the RSL man said, 'He was a good sergeant.' It seemed such a simple and yet resonating sentence that it brought the tremors to the surface. But chiefly, movements of grief remained in the interior of the planet, the planet Earth and the planet me. I apologise in an age when depression is routinely announced, often with good intentions, often as an excuse, to say that six weeks after my father's death—in the exact middle of the Sydney Olympics, as it happened—I was overtaken by disabling depression. The interesting thing about depression is that it is seen as an absence of wellbeing, but in fact it is a presence in its own right. It drives any energy or creativity or intent out of a person, and cancels the future in a different way from death. I may be deluding myself, but it seemed to me to arise from a death inadequately acknowledged, my father's death. Not working, since work was impossible, my father's purposeful final changing of the shirt reproached me. He had always worked. I had nosedived out of it. If there was a contest, I now knew who was the better man.

It's almost unnecessary for a writer to say he was a hopeless kid. Writers have generally been on the margins of the playground and on the margins of the sort of academic achievements that make mothers glow. So, ex officio, I was a hopeless kid, and I do apologise if you've already heard this sort of tale from others. Part of the hopelessness was that I was asthmatic at a stage of medical history when there was no treatment for it at all. To go within five yards of privet or paspalum was to incur a night's gasping. In those nights, my mother was company and comfort. My mother and I were like partners in crime, for doctors, unable to treat the disease, blamed it on supposedly overemotional mothers and pampered children.

So that was strike one. Send the kids out to play, and I would turn up at the door after forty minutes gasping, letting down myself, my playmates and, as I saw from the shadow of anxiety on her face, my mother. Since this condition put me in her frequent company at all hours, and since she was the one who tried by every means to get air into me, she became associated with free breath.

Then—bring in the violins!—there was my scholastic ineptitude. To go along with the off-putting mucus of the perpetually allergic child, I had a capacity, unmatched in my class, to spill ink. (These were the days when you *could* blot your copybook.) I could not even get right the place they'd sent my father. I told the nun he'd gone to 'the Middle West'. I wanted to be the kid who took home to his mother the rubber-stamped stars for good work. Instead I took home letters asking her to front Sister Felicitas to hear complaints about those half-dried ink-blots—and my total lack of attention.

Failure bound me irrevocably to my mother by our shared dreams of validation. Because even then I noticed something peculiar and unrepayable: she never lost her fierce faith in me.

Finally, in the process of making me a mother's boy, my father was away for two and a half years continuously, and if you count the bush camps he had to spend time in, longer still. My mother had extra time to try to make me a potential reader and studier, and to believe—despite all the evidence of my incompetence—that that's what I would become.

Mind you, I would like tentatively to question whether a mother's boy is such a bad thing to become. Why is it implicitly okay to be a father's boy, no matter what sort of oaf or thug the father might happen to be, and suspect to be a mother's? Of course, it depends on the mother. My amiable father was away, but in the meantime, despite all, I was certainly getting the Rugby League and male biffo side of my nature from school.

I was getting the digger side from my father by way of the Australian Comforts Fund cake tins full of Italian and German memorabilia fetched from a dwindling pocket of German and Italian defence in North Africa. I got it too from boxing films, and did a lot of clumsy boxing with other boys. I had no allergic reaction to boxing, especially if the fight took place far enough from paspalum. One arranged fight on Parramatta Road lasted more than half an hour, and the grocers from Moran & Cato's and the butchers' men came out of their shops and barracked and whistled. When I told her about it, my mother wept. She had seen the limitations of brawling in the streets of Kempsey, how men said of my father, 'He was a great five-eighth, but he used to come the knuckle.'

Redemption—the chance to gratify the parents—arrived one day when I was hitting puberty, and suddenly understood Pythagoras' theorem at a gulp, like a revelation. This did not mean that I could wander like a dazzling child through the gardens of Euclid, algebra and trigonometry. But it was like the breaking of a cerebral logjam. All at once I could write essays, comprehend a little history, understand Latin subjunctives. I found I could play sport, too, and thus reflected dimly my father's record. My parents believed me to be on the way to becoming 'a professional man', a lawyer or a doctor, the only kinds of men whom they had seen survive the Depression. Now the skimping in order to afford the school fees was paying a dividend—a modest but increasing one in my case, a spectacular one in my little brother's, as his later life in ground-breaking medicine would prove.

And then, of course, I buggered it all up again. It is sometimes too readily assumed that old-style Catholics desired one of their sons to become a priest. Mine did not. Visiting an alcoholic relative in a sanatorium, my mother noticed how many alcoholic priests populated the place, a phenomenon she attributed to loneliness. But I developed an irrational and stubborn intention to become a priest. I could sense a huge reluctance in my parents, but I had the ill-informed self-confidence that it would all work out splendidly.

It didn't. After some five to six years, within sight of ordination, I left the place. My mother had ordered the caterer for my ordination breakfast and had to cancel. I did not have the words to explain what drove me from the place—loss of faith in general, and certainly loss of faith in the kind of men who ran the place. I could not explain either that I was mentally and emotionally exhausted, because we did not have the words for that in those days, and because I somehow believed that saying it would be the final blow to all my parents' residual hopes. I also could not explain why I could not study anything more, and even if I could, was not in a position to undertake full-time study.

Naturally enough, and with some justice, I felt a massive failure and, as in the ink-blot days, had somehow situated myself again on the fringes. Most of my seminary class, when priests, would themselves leave their parishes and marry. Many of them worked in the parole service, and in other human welfare areas, and are among some of the finest humans I've known. But when I left I did not know that this would happen.

So I had to get a job and make things up to the household. I was twenty-three or so, making decisions that should have been made years before. The worst thing was that, yea, like a mother in a movie, my mother still believed in me, and to a degree that nearly made my soul itch. Because the debt I wanted to pay could never be acquitted—that was obvious.

When I began writing in the summer holidays of 1962–63, and then got published the following year, I started to get back into pleasing-the-parents territory. At the same time I ruined it a bit by saying that the church was as capable of corruption as an insurance company might be. This, a blatant fact now, was considered then the height not only of blasphemy, but of heresy. Still my parents did not renounce me. Though observant Catholics, they were rather left-wing by impulse and in social terms, as many of their generation were, and so they knew, as many intelligent adult Catholics even then did, the limitations of the church's probity and much-vaunted compassion. But I didn't understand that as well as I do now.

As time passed, and my stance and my books grew a little less manic, I was delighted to be paying them back with a certain degree of fame (or as some would perhaps more justly have it, notoriety). I felt that the church thing divided me from many of my clan—though they didn't worry about it as much as I thought—but the time was coming when I could help my parents in material ways, and in the way of giving them experiences that were worthy of them. Was there a tendency to show the old man that I was the warrior now, that I could come the knuckle with the world? There might have been. But they generously considered me a good son, and although that was what I wanted, I perversely hated to hear them say it. I knew the truth. How much ground there was to make up.

Interestingly, to be able to help them financially, despite their pride, was a matter of simple joy. These seemed strangely less complicated transactions than matters of achievement and the inducing of parental pride. Secretly to plan holidays they wouldn't otherwise have taken, and surprising them with tickets, was something my wife and daughters and I did with glee. One could say with *selfish* glee, but if so that's a modest taint. The cries of wonder would be followed by cries about our economic recklessness (accurately diagnosed), and then by their resignation to the joy of it. 'Well, we might as well go, I suppose, or it'll go to waste.' God forbid though that, while away, they would ever add an iota to the bill by taking anything from the mini-bar—in my father's eyes the mini-bar was an obscene little shrine to Mammon, designed by 'thieving capitalist bastards'.

My late brother was also a payer-back, but between him and me—we were eight years apart, after all—there existed no trace of sibling competition. His generosity seemed more automatic and less complicated by competing motives than mine, though that might have been an illusion. Since his babyhood he had done nothing to bemuse his parents. He had been an uncomplicatedly brilliant child, student, medical student, doctor and specialist. He worked in the public system, in which he believed. He was never depressed or depleted. He was a very liberal Catholic, and at the same time, to mention just one achievement, designed the operating theatres at the Children's Hospital and a means of extracting toxic anaesthesia fumes from them. He introduced dozens of enlightened reforms which would earn him an Order of Australia. Fortunately it was after my parents died that he was claimed too early by the beast, cancer.

While the monster's hand lay relatively quiescent on him, we went for walks in the bush and meals, and even a trip to

Turkey, and ended up talking about our parents, of course, and our reaction to their deaths. He calmly said he wished he'd been a better son. This from a man who had them over to every grandchild concert, and to dinners—an acid test!—to which he invited other friends. But he confessed the extent to which they could annoy him, and now he regretted that annoyance. As we always can when it's someone else, I told him off for misreading himself. He'd just have to face the fact he'd been a wonderful, an exemplary child. I told him that there were things my mother could say which would transform me, in my sixties, into a sullen fourteen-year-old. But it struck me that if a man like my brother felt this loss, the loss of a chance to adjust the scales, child to parent, then the whole world must.

In our family we were all saved from that double death of the parent, where some time before the physical extinction there is a retreat into veils of un-memory, and the loss of the capacity to put a name to the items of the earth and to read a face. At the age of ninety-four my mother was still enjoying glasses of wine, conversing from her chair at clan reunions, and calling me to see whether I had read the feature article on the Horn of Africa, Barack Obama's health plan, or the latest shift in asylum-seeker policy in that morning's *Herald*. I knew I faced a probing discussion on the issue. She had plenty of opinions, and they were unexpected ones for what people would call 'her demographic'. Despite her saying of nightly prayers, she believed in the ordination of women and a married clergy. She was appalled by what had been done to Aborigines and asylum-seekers, and had particular contempt for the fundamentalist position that being gay was a 'lifestyle choice'.

My father was clear-headed until the morphine, and similarly only when the first dose of morphine entered my mother's bloodstream was there mental confusion. She kept telling me that she knew I had friends in another room, she could hear them talking, and I ought to go and join them. The painful imputation seemed to me to be, 'Go on, you have done your duty, now go and talk to people more akin to you.' She had always regretted her limited education and was aware all her life that only going as far as the Primary Final (Year 6) at Kempsey convent had restricted her opportunities in the world. The fact that she could write better than most arts graduates and read more coherently did not console her. I kept on saying that there were no friends waiting in another room, and listing the relatives who were on their way to see her, and explaining that the morphine was unsettling her. But the thing about morphine is that it imbues the patient with a new set of convictions and senses, and might, in however addled a way, let out what has to this point not been uttered. Then unconsciousness took her, and all the chains of hope and ambition and reckless affection and doubt were broken.

For her. But as I show here, not for me.

ESTHER JEAN

SUSAN DUNCAN

ON THE DAY MY MOTHER turned ninety years old, torrential rain pounded out of a growling black sky, gale-force winds whipped the sea into a roiling frenzy and getting to our water-access home was borderline life-threatening for anyone under fifty. Naturally, she refused to cancel her party even though it meant thirty guests, including her 'boyfriend', who was ninety-nine years old and wheelchair-bound, had to make a rugged ferry crossing. If he—and all the octogenarians—survived the disembarkation at the Lovett Bay wharf, then climbing eighty-eight slippery sandstone steps to our home, which sits on a high, rough hill in Sydney's Pittwater, would probably seem like a doddle.

'You could switch venues,' I suggested hopefully, visualising heart attacks, broken bones and instant onsets of fatal pneumonia.

'No way! People our age don't get the chance to have many adventures,' she said blithely.

The party went ahead. Most of the guests made it, soaked

to the skin, their bodies shaking uncontrollably from the effort. And yet, despite the horror conditions, not a soul complained. Not even the almost-centenarian who spent the afternoon encased snugly in a faux-fur blanket by my mother's side. Some of them even relished the challenge and stood in the hallway to be hosed with hot air from a couple of woefully inadequate hairdryers, their eyes sparkling, laughing with what must have been a rare sense of achievement—although admittedly no one later danced to the music from the band my mother insisted I hire for the event.

Early the following week, when two guests died (in their sleep) and one was hospitalised with life-threatening pneumonia (his family was called to say their final farewells but, thank God, he survived), my mother, who didn't even suffer a sniffle, waved her hand dismissively: 'Better to go out with a bang,' she said. 'Oh, and by the way, I like the jacket you loaned me so I think I'll keep it. But your trousers were too long so you can have *them* back.'

My mother's name is Esther Jean and she was born in a two-bedroom weatherboard house in Dalley Street, Northcote, Victoria, on 21 March, 1921, delivered with only a small amount of difficulty by an old cousin called Anne—never Annie—who was the local midwife. The name Esther was chosen for its biblical significance and, theoretically at least, to imbue a sense of righteousness. Jean, as she was universally known, was meant to add a little pizzazz. From all accounts, pizzazz dominated and my mother boasts she was engaged twenty-two times before the age of twenty-one. My brother John and I arbitrarily decided to call her 'Esther' as soon as we were old enough to drop 'Mum'. I have no idea why.

When Esther was still a baby, her parents—dark-haired and diminutive Henrietta, who feared God and wielded superstition like a sword, and rakish, immoral Felix Parker, who'd been a courier in France in World War I and often boasted he'd rubbed shoulders with royalty when he picked up the handkerchief of the King of Belgium (who happened to be passing)—moved house and opened a fruit shop in Johnston Street, Abbotsford. They quickly built a thriving business.

In her own words, Esther Jean was 'not a nice child'. 'When I was four years old and not long after my twin sisters were born, all I wanted for Christmas was my own axe,' she told me. 'I was given a doll. So to make the point as clear as day, I snapped off the doll's head. Then I went outside onto the street, which was a very, very busy thoroughfare, and danced for pennies. I wanted the money, but really, I think I liked the attention more. My parents were horrified but I didn't care. Actually, I did quite well until they carted me away.'

After her parents fell for a shady con job and lost the fruit shop, my mother shifted her stage from the cracked pavement to the slightly risqué Tivoli Theatre, where she auditioned for the chorus line. Once again, her parents were appalled, but they needn't have worried; she made the shortlist but not the cast. Soon after, she became a nurse's aide in the Australian Army and landed in a shattered Darwin six days after the Japanese bombed the still-fledgling country town. She was wonderful with the patients and even today, at the age of ninety-two, she has enormous compassion and patience for anyone who is ill. I used to think her dedicated nursing—sometimes of strangers—was her way of building up credits for the afterlife (in which she firmly believes). Then I saw the joy—and purpose—she found in preparing and arranging little lunch platters day after day to tempt the dulled appetite of a sick friend, and I (grudgingly) had to give her credit for kindness and care.

My older brother John and I were born almost five years apart after she married my father, a great shambling, gentle man who reached for a cigarette on the bedside table before he opened his eyes in the morning and consistently drank a minimum of four longnecks every evening. He was devoted to Esther and (as I found out only recently) thanked her for looking after his cancer-ridden mother by buying her a lush fur coat that to this day, moth-eaten and mouldy, hangs in her wardrobe. Trouble was, she told me in a rare moment of candour, he loved a drink as much as he loved her and she'd never been good at sharing. It was never an ideal relationship, but how many truly are?

My mother never struck us in anger—well, my brother once caught a leather belt on the back of his legs when he couldn't find his shoes and was about to set off to school barefoot. After the whack, Esther sobbed and sobbed until my completely unfazed brother advised her never to take up the strap again because it upset her too much. Anyway, she easily ruled her two tearaway, sunburned country kids without having to resort to anything more than a look so cold and dark it made us flinch.

'Snow', as my father referred to John, was always wise beyond his years and my mother adored him, which was the way of most women of her generation who, if they outlived their spouses, were dependent on sons for their survival. In many ways, my soft-hearted, clever, larrikin brother was the nail that held the sometimes volatile Duncan family together, especially after my father died and my mother, a financial dill pickle (her words, not mine), tried to fend for herself and ran through every penny my father had left her within a couple of years. Often my brother stepped in with cash in hand, which Esther inevitably blew on a new outfit or hat instead of the electricity bill it was meant for. If nothing else, she was an expert at living in the moment, which she has only lately begun to admit meant she was often her own worst enemy.

From my own childhood perspective, our early years were vaguely chaotic and driven mostly by my father's drinking and his love of gambling. I remember lean Christmases occasionally, and Easters when the only chocolate we were given came from understanding neighbours in the Bonegilla migrant camp on the New South Wales–Victorian border where my father was a supply officer. No matter how slow the horses though, my mother—as far as I can remember—never missed her weekly appointment with the hairdresser. Like a born show pony, no matter what frantic mess lay behind the scenes, she never failed to come to life and perform brilliantly in front of an audience. The little dancer toe-tapping the pavement for pennies never really died in her.

Carelessly certain of her own physical beauty, my mother measured all other women's worth by the same yardstick. I failed to meet nearly every one of her rigid criteria. Too tall with red hair and freckles, a large nose, not enough chin, I was plain-looking by even the kindest standards. In another age, I might have been the daughter who entered the convent or who stayed home to care for elderly parents.

'You've always thought I was disappointed in you because you weren't beautiful,' Esther said the other day. 'But you always had such *character*.' And I can't help smiling at the irony: it was my mother's dissatisfaction with me that taught me to distrust praise or compliments (her own rare approval was always delivered with a painful sting in the tail), that made me try harder and harder, that led me to achieve far more than I ever dreamed possible. *Character?* I shrugged and let it go. Why focus on the blade? At least she has always been honest and so I've never had to suffer the long plunge downwards from the shaky scaffolding of false praise.

After my brother died slowly and painfully from a rare form of cancer at the age of forty-six, she was stuck with me and, equally, I was tied to her. By now, I was old and acute enough to suspect that my mother, who publicly shouted her love and pride in me, was in fact shamelessly self-absorbed, compulsively manipulative and downright competitive. Am I being fair? Probably not entirely, but then children never are, are they? In an odd way, we are more spectators than participants in the mechanics of family life, neither responsible for providing the infrastructure on which everything depends, nor even liable for our wellbeing until we are old enough to make rational decisions. Until then, our parents lay down the rules and we arrogantly blame them for every knock and failure. It took a long while to understand that what I considered her worst characteristics were not her weaknesses, but her strengths.

The truth, too, is that a child's perception of a parent is utterly different from an outsider's. Not so long ago, I received a letter from a childhood playmate. He wrote of the warmth and hilarity of our household, of his astonishment that my brother and I were to be found carousing in our parents' toast-crumbed bed late on a Sunday morning. In his formal Germanic home, such behaviour was unthinkable. He envied us. It was a revelation to me.

My mother was capable—and still is—of the most enormous acts of kindness and generosity. She agreed to my father's uncle coming to live with us (actually, he came for a two-week holiday and didn't leave until he died more than a decade later). She looked after him as dementia turned him into a bed-wetting and paranoid old man with increasingly violent tendencies (he once hid behind the bedroom door and tried to knock her out). Did I help? Of course not.

Almost ten years ago, and long before we decided to accept our mutual shortcomings without comment, I moved my mother from her distant home to a nearby retirement village. She was eighty-two years old and had had a couple of falls in quick succession, breaking first one wrist and then the other. She was showing signs of barely coping—nests of unopened mail piled around the house, dust an inch thick, a backyard littered with pots and pans burned beyond salvation. She had begun to rely on strangers to reverse her car out of shopping-centre car parks before she could drive off; she locked herself out of her own house so frequently her neighbour cut a hole in a window so she could climb in and out without calling on him for help. She'd started to fake increasingly serious illnesses in a bid for attention and, as a result, was endangering her health by swallowing drugs for phantom symptoms. My mother, whom I'd always regarded as invincible, was no longer getting old—

she *was* old. She looked at me with rabbit-scared eyes when I suggested a retirement village: 'I know where everything is here, so forget it,' she said, but agreed to the move with relief once I had walked her through a small white unit set in magical gardens with a cheeky water dragon on the balcony balustrade.

When I packed her home, I was shocked to find piles of magazines I'd once worked for stacked inside cupboards. Shocked because when I occasionally rang her to mention a cover story and to ask with a little pride (which she always said came right before a fall) if she might like to read it, she was never interested. 'I don't read that stuff. Anyway, the magazine is too expensive. People will stop buying it soon.' And yet, when I called in to her local grocery store one time, the Greek owner told me: 'Your mother is proud of you, she . . . busts with pride!' I smiled politely, not believing a word—until I found those old magazines. Every cover story I could remember and other less flamboyant assignments were thumbed through and then hidden from sight like pornography. Maybe my mother thought a little praise would go straight to my head and ruin me forever, but she could do no harm by boasting out loud to others. Like her own mother, she's always been a deeply superstitious woman. Don't walk under ladders. Never cut your fingernails on a Friday. If a painting falls off the wall someone will die. New shoes on the table bring bad luck. Saying goodbye means you'll never meet again. Lilies in the house bring death to your door. *Don't tempt the gods by praising those you love or they will take them from you.*

One day, when I visited her in her new home, I tackled her about the stash of magazines. 'You told me you never bought them because they were too expensive.'

'People insisted on giving them to me,' she snapped.

'Did you actually read any of my stories?'

'Oh, I can't remember,' she said, as if a compliment might kill her. It was the first time I ever wondered whether she might envy instead of cherish (as parents supposedly do) my small successes.

I wondered, too, if she was hard on me because she saw too much of herself in my childhood recklessness, my early overabundance of confidence. Perhaps she set about knocking it out of me in a bid to keep me safe. I could ask her, of course. I'm not sure she knows the truth, though, and even if she did, whether she would admit it. But now that we are equally grey-haired and the passion for combat is waning in both of us, there *are* changes in the air, moments of candour and confession.

The other day she suddenly said, 'I think I was jealous of John's wife. He was my son, after all, and I found it difficult to see him with another woman.'

'Blind Freddy could have told you that,' I responded. Our father, by the time John and I were teenagers, had descended so deep into the bottle he would never find his way back to the surface. So my brother was the one who took my mother to glamorous restaurants, bought her expensive clothes, whipped her away for weekends in Sydney or Adelaide and sent her shopping while he went to the races. When he married, the whirl that lifted her out of the dull flatline of her beer-sodden suburbia came to an abrupt end. Outraged, my mother tried so hard to foul the marriage that my brother's wife banned her from the house until Esther came to her senses and let her son get on with building his own life.

'He loved me, though. He really did. I know he did,' Esther says. And I squirm in my seat. The words are somehow unmaternal. Unfitting. Should I remind her how she tried to undo my first marriage? I didn't see it, of course. I never recognised the self-interest so cunningly disguised as maternal concern. Not even after my late husband spelled it out in words of one syllable. 'She wants the best for me,' I insisted. 'She wants the lot for her,' he insisted. But still, I couldn't reject a lifetime's conditioning that, in all things, my mother must come first and she had my best interests at heart.

And you know, I believe she truly did. She wanted my brother and me to excel, to be the best, not only because she planned to tag along on our coattails, but because she wanted us to have a better life than hers. It all went screwy, of course, because as much as she desired our success, when we achieved any small measure she envied it, even occasionally tried to sabotage it.

I dreamed, in those first weeks of her life in the retirement village, of putting aside rancour and finally being a good daughter, but to my shame I seized on any excuse to back away from full responsibility for her emotional wellbeing. In truth, I failed to understand how hard it was for a woman in her eighties to make such a massive change. I expected her to be up and away with a single bound, because in her idiosyncratic way, my mother has always been fearless. Or at least, a genius at disguising her frailties—mostly with humour, and with anger only very rarely. I waited in vain for her to flick her skirt flirtatiously, grin almost lasciviously and get on with it. Instead, she retreated to her small white unit to the point where her concerned neighbour suggested burning the floral sofa might be the only way to get her up and about. When I tried to help it was in a high-handed, bullying way that didn't do either of us much good.

Not long ago, she announced that she had no fear of death. I didn't believe her for a second. Who doesn't fear death—or the eternal mystery of it—at least on some level? I have often wondered, too, if the reason my mother (who believes firmly in the idea of heaven and hell) has lived for ninety-two years is simply because she is desperately afraid of what she would call Judgment Day. 'I have secrets,' she told me once, so quietly I almost missed the words. I sat next to her like a cross-examiner until she revealed all. Well, enough, anyway, for me to know that by today's standards most of her secrets were paltry. The one or two that had more far-reaching consequences she excused as selfless acts to help one person or another. Which is the way, I suspect, most of us come to grips with our blacker and most ignoble moments. Despite her rationalisations, these acts—large and small—have governed her idea of self-worth for most of her life. One way or another, as I'm sure she would agree, we pay for our sins.

That day, the conversation about death continued for a while, and she explained that one of the reasons she was unafraid was because she believed John would be very pleased to see her and her husband had been waiting a long time for her arrival. 'He spoiled me rotten, you know, although I never realised it at the time.'

Uncharitably, I couldn't help wondering whether one of the reasons my father drank was because he had realised that no matter how much he lavished on my mother, it would never be enough. It's a thought that brings me back to the idea of self-worth, of course, and that dreadfully destructive combination of huge ego and low self-esteem that afflicts so many of us. My mother's bucket could never be filled because why would anyone give her anything unless it was worthless?

Once a week, I do what I consider to be my duty no matter how rancorous our current relationship and take her out to lunch. Her first comments when we meet are invariably personal: 'Is your iron broken?' or 'When you next go to the hairdresser see if they can do something about your dry hair.' Now, instead of reacting or burning up inside, I simply nod. Disengagement, I have learned, is a powerful tool.

Regardless of raging storms or chronic heatwaves, we drive to the beach at Mona Vale for a picnic lunch. There the crowds are young and healthy, the surf a feast of power and indomitability, and without stepping outside the car and reaching for her walking frame, my mother can get her fill of a physical world that is now way beyond even her imagination of her old self. The car picnic is her choice. When I asked her why, she replied, 'Because I've got you captive.' But really, I suspect it is to avoid admitting defeat. Getting in and out of the car is difficult, even a short walk to a restaurant exhausts her. Understanding my mother, I have finally learned, means fleshing out the subtext and ferreting out the motive.

Just a few days ago, I told her I'd been unable to find two leather armchairs like her red ones. 'Well, it won't be long before you get mine anyway,' she replied, gearing up for a round of emotional blackmail.

I pounced hard and fast. 'They're the wrong colour. And anyway, it'll take a vet's needle to see you off once and for all.'

Caught out, she laughed from deep in her belly.

'You realise we've both got a shockingly black sense of humour?' she replied, still grinning.

'Who said I was joking?' And then we both laughed so long and loud the man in the panel van parked next to us wound up his window.

'When were you happiest?' I asked one stormy day when surging grey seas created by a low-pressure system and a king tide crashed against cliff faces and frothed on red sand. It was the time of year the whales make their migrations northwards from the South Pole so I scanned the billowing water for signs of those great glossy barnacled bodies emerging like small islands to catch their breath. The sight of one, I knew, would give her intense pleasure.

'When we lived at Bonegilla,' she replied, without hesitation. It was the 1950s, she was the beautiful blonde and extroverted wife who shone brightly in the small pond of Bonegilla Migrant Camp, where the Australians were at the top of the social order and treated like royalty, which suited her perfectly. 'I wish I'd realised at the time it was as good as it was going to get.'

'Perhaps it's your youth you mourn more than the era,' I suggested.

'Maybe,' she admitted.

She was working her way through twelve lush, plump and musk-scented Pacific oysters. Six potato scallops awaited in a white paper bag torn a little, to let the steam escape to stop the batter from going soggy. I ate a meat pie with tomato sauce. The menu never varies. I wonder if our choices say a fair bit about our personalities.

I was reminded of the morning after my sixteenth birthday party in the country pub she and my father bought after quitting the camp. My mother sat on a kitchen stool and voraciously scoffed a huge hessian bagful of leftover unshucked oysters. She was forty-six years old and in her prime.

On Saturday nights, a white-haired, arthritic pianist called Gil (short for Gillespie) rocked along with a repertoire of golden oldies that romanticised the camaraderie of both the world wars. After a few whiskies for courage, my mother would take the microphone and sing a solo in a clear soprano voice. The kid on the footpath once again. Fired up by the limelight. In her prime until it took far too many whiskies too often to find her old hubris. 'I sold the pub behind your father's back,' she confessed. 'It would have killed him in the end.' What she won't admit is that she was falling deeper and deeper into the bottle herself and it was more an act of self-preservation than concern for her husband. 'He never forgave me, you know.' No. I didn't know.

One day, the village manager tells me my mother set off the fire alarm in her unit at two-fifty am. 'She was making toast,' the manager explains. 'Why would she be making toast in the small hours of the morning?'

I can think of a million reasons but I shrug silently, knowing I will have to remove the toaster because the fire brigade charge seven hundred and fifty dollars for every false alarm, and this is already her second offence (if that is the right word).

At our next picnic at the beach, I tell my mother, 'I'll have to confiscate the toaster, you know.'

'Don't you dare!' Her eyes flash.

'No choice. Sorry.'

'I'll buy another one,' she says defiantly, as she slides an oyster into her mouth—Sydney Rocks this time.

'I can't help you if you won't help yourself.'

And she backs off without firing another shot. It is frightening, this sudden acquiescence. Horrified, I watch her lower lip tremble, her hand begin to shake violently.

To soften the blow, I add, 'I'll bring it back in a couple of weeks. We just need to show that we're doing our best.'

'Yes,' she says, but we both know the toaster is gone forever.

'Do you remember,' I say, to change the subject in a way I hope is pleasant, 'when you taught John and me to play word games on long car trips? Listen to the sound of them, you told us, don't worry about the meaning, pick the most beautiful-sounding words in the world.'

'Did I?'

'I immediately shouted out that beautiful was my word. Even as I said it, I understood it was clunky. No, no, I said quickly, not beautiful. Lake. Lake is my word! I think that was the moment I fell in love with language. Way back then.'

'You were lucky. You had brains. I never did.'

'You're rat-cunning, though.' It is out before I have time to register that my mother has just paid me one of the few genuine compliments I can remember and that *rat-cunning*, meant as a simple fact, could be construed as cruel.

'Oh yes,' she admits, unoffended. 'Not that it's ever done me any good.'

When she was just a couple of months shy of eighty-eight years old she fainted and was rushed to hospital. As it turned out, her heart was failing. The doctor mentioned heart surgery. I wanted to know the downside for a woman her age. He made me ask every question in front of her, which I doubt I'll ever forgive him for. Did she really need to know the percentage risk of emerging from surgery a mentally crippled wreck? In the end, he turned to my mother and asked, 'So shall we operate or not?'

'Go for it!' she said. 'Your brother and dad will just have to wait.' And I, I thought selfishly, will have to pick up the pieces if it all goes awry. Then I asked myself what I would do in the same situation. Probably make the same choice. Another day, when they are fast running out, would have to glow like pure gold.

She had a triple bypass and a heart valve replaced on Christmas Eve. When I went to see her on Christmas Day, she was lying in bed with a million tubes crisscrossing her papery skin, eyes closed, her breathing ragged. I sat and wept. Despite the fact that we still have an uncanny ability to step off on the wrong foot when we are together, despite our massive differences and our reluctance to see the best in each other, there is no question about love. It is deep, abiding and, yes, unconditional. Neither of us would ever, could ever, abandon the other. My mother, with the glint of emotional victory in her eye, would say, *Blood is thicker than water*. And she would be right. If she dies before me, I suspect I will miss her quite dreadfully. Now that we are both grey-haired with deeply fissured faces and we have more or less called a truce, or at least stopped being offended by the kind of remarks family are allowed and forgiven for making, who else could I sit alongside in a car at the beach who would understand the unspoken subtext of every conversation?

As my mother shuffles towards her centenary and I walk behind prodding her (not always gently) ever onwards, we have learned to accept who we both are. Some might call it *peace* but *truce* is closer to the truth.

A couple of days later when the tube was removed from her throat and she could speak, she opened her eyes when I entered her room and a faint glimmer of the old shine flooded them. 'They've guaranteed me ten years,' she croaked. 'But I reckon I'll be able to push it out to fifteen.'

I counted the years on my fingers. 'So I'll be looking after you until I'm seventy-five,' I said, with a mock groan.

She managed a grin. 'I win,' she said. And we laughed because it is a Duncan tradition to laugh in the face of adversity, a tradition she's instilled in me since birth and that has saved me from despair more times than I can bear to think about.

Last week, when the seas were so calm they barely moved and the surfers bobbed aimlessly on their boards, my mother told me again how much her son, my brother who died far too young, had loved her. On this day, I am late to collect her after an appointment, so we sit with just our coffees and a couple of pastries. I'd offered her the full oyster menu, but she'd had lunch with all the other village inmates and at her age, she informed me primly, the appetite shrinks. 'So only one potato scallop next week?' I asked, teasing. 'Perhaps three,' she replied, knowing I will continue to buy six.

She stares at the sea, the sky. I point out a couple of people on horseback but she can't see them.

'Would you like to get out of the car?' I ask, because she has always loved horses and was an accomplished rider in her day.

'No. I'll take your word for it.'

I look at her closely. 'Are you feeling okay?'

'I'm not about to drop off the perch, if that's what you mean, and even if I were, I've told you: death doesn't scare me.'

'I think it does,' I bat back, expecting to get a rise out of her that will indicate she really is all right.

'What would you know?' she says dismissively.

'I've been hearing you're at death's door since you were forty-nine years old. For a woman who thought she wouldn't make it to fifty, you're doing okay.'

Again, she fails to take the bait. Instead she says, 'You have no idea how much my body hurts. Even when I lie still, it feels like rats gnawing at my bones or pushing needles into them. You can live too long, you know.'

We return in silence to the village. I remove her walker from the boot, pat her back as she heads into the grand sitting room where a fire burns brightly and a crowd of women, crowned with white hair styled in the precise waves of the 1950s, are busy with crafts. '*My* daughter is coming for me tomorrow,' boasts one of the knitters as we pass. And I am quite sure, even if my mother never admits it, that she does the same.

Back in the car, I head for home, thinking about death, feeling terribly, terribly sad. Then I remember: my mother has an incredibly strong competitive streak. She will do her best to outlive me. And I am cheered enormously by the thought.

LUMINOSITY

NIKKI BARROWCLOUGH

'I saw the sky.'

My mother whispered these words from her hospital bed a few days before she died. They weren't her final words, but after that she barely spoke again. She was sleeping as she slipped towards death.

Four years have passed, and I'm still haunted by that moment.

Why is it that my mother's life had to end so sadly, so horribly and, for someone who'd suffered a long, traumatic stay in hospital only two years earlier, with no joy left to her? She seemed to have been in hospital forever, and for her that was the same as being in exile—banished to a room and a bed not her own, her only glimpse of the 'outside world' through a doorway past which she saw only the constant traffic of strangers.

But her eyes were turned towards the doorway every morning. She was waiting for us to arrive. They followed us to the doorway each night when we left. Once, I tiptoed back to make sure she had closed her eyes. I feared she would be weeping, but it was worse than that. I saw my mother staring straight ahead with an expression of total despair.

Then came the day when, even though she was frail beyond belief, someone gave an order to take my mother to another part of the hospital for a scan, which meant they had to wheel her across the quadrangle; and for a few precious moments, lying on her back, she had looked into the blue and the joy was still in her eyes when she whispered those words a few hours later.

I saw the sky.

But with those four simple words she was also mourning the life she knew was now lost to her.

We took her fresh flowers every other day, placing them in vases around her bed so that they filled her gaze. But there was no blocking out where she was. She had so feared going back into hospital. We knew she was longing to be at home with my father, having her glass of brandy before dinner, or concocting one of her wonderful puddings, or driving to the ocean with him to sit for a while and watch the horizon, now that their sailing days were over.

In my memories, she's always outside: in her garden, or picking the herbs she grew in a series of glorious old stone pots, or laughing on the deck of my father's boat on Sunday afternoons, wearing huge sunglasses and with her trousers rolled up to her knees as she hauled in another fish; my father, who invariably caught nothing, always used to say that the fish found her.

'My girl,' he called her all through their marriage.

'My girl,' he says now, as he sits in his chair by the window, watching the street from the third-floor apartment where he has lived since the house in which he lived with my mother was sold. He wears a faraway expression and can be silent for hours.

The small, narrow street where he lives disappears around a corner. You can never see who's approaching until someone comes into view. I don't think for a moment that my father is imagining my mother coming around the corner, but I'm absolutely certain that he's reliving their years together.

My mother went into hospital for the second to last time after she'd tripped and fallen down a flight of steep concrete steps outside the back door of the house. She was rushed by ambulance to the hospital, moaning in pain and unable to speak. My father went into shock.

But it wasn't the injuries from the fall that saw her lying incarcerated in a hospital intensive care unit for the best part of a year.

One morning, while she was still in the ward, my sister found her in excruciating pain and, despite pleading with a nurse to call Mum's doctor, nothing was done. By the time someone did take notice of my mother's plunging blood pressure and medical staff rushed to her bedside, an undiagnosed ulcer in her stomach had burst. It was almost too late to save her.

Her recovery took ages and she was grief-stricken for much of the time—and frightened. When at last she began to improve, the nurses would push her in a wheelchair onto the small concrete terrace outside ICU, where she would sit, her eyes covered in hospital-issued wraparound sunglasses: immobile, silent. She never spoke. Sometimes she didn't look like my mother at all.

I think she had taken herself off somewhere mentally in order to bear what she was going through.

And then she really did start getting better and, after a period of rehabilitation, she finally went home—back to my father, to her garden, to their beloved routine.

But Mum had been left greatly weakened as a result of these awful events and as the months went by, she began very gently to fade.

Soon she was too weak to do much more than sit in her chair and sleep—although sometimes she asked to sit in the sun on the front veranda, where she could see passers-by—'Because I like to see movement,' she always said. In the evening she'd struggle to finish her meal and then painfully, slowly, start pushing her walker back along the hall to the bedroom, always with Dad in tow.

'Look up, darling,' he'd say. But my mother walked with her head bowed.

In the huge box of black-and-white photographs which were somehow never put into albums, there are many photos of my mother as a beautiful young woman in evening dress, off to a ball; or at the ball, on my father's arm. Or dancing. There's also one of her walking along the beach in a white swimsuit, which I always called Mum's Marilyn Monroe photo.

We kept her at home in her own bed until she became so frail that we knew we had to call her doctor—who came immediately, took one look at Mum and said she had to go into hospital: she had pneumonia.

I wanted to bring in nurses, and oxygen, and whatever else was needed to keep her where I knew she felt safe.

To my infinite regret we gave in at mention of the word 'pneumonia'. Later that day, just before dusk, she was visibly shocked when two big, burly men walked into the bedroom and, without warning, lifted her in their brisk, unsentimental fashion onto an ambulance trolley bed.

Within minutes the paramedics had pushed the trolley bed down the hall and through the dining room, past the living room and through the little entrance hall, out the front door and up the driveway towards the ambulance parked in the street.

This is the other memory that haunts me. Mum lying propped up against the pillows with anguish in her eyes—wide open for the first time in weeks—as she stared back at her home, receding from her sight.

She knew. She knew.

I still try to push from my mind the worst of what followed: the ghastliness of watching her trapped yet again by a hospital routine and especially by the way the end of her life was reorganised, recast and then made remote by the medicalisation of death.

Shouldn't the end of a life be given the same status as a rare fragment of music, so beautiful that it makes you halt in your tracks? And yes, of course we should ease someone's dying with medical intervention to stop pain and suffering, and there are certain practicalities of routine that are inevitable in a hospital. Nor do I mean to suggest that we should be unrealistic or even romantic about death: it's not romantic.

But the end of a life *is* momentous. The end of a parent's life changes your own life forever. You've been set free, and yet in some inexplicable way you're more bound than ever to the parent who died because of memory; and death gives memory added power.

My mother's essential sweetness—despite her mystifying rages when we were growing up—a sweetness which we, her children, so arrogant in our twenties, dismissed as naivety, is the quality that shines brightest whenever I think of her now.

I wrote a brief eulogy that I was unable to read out at her funeral, and I carry those lines in the pages of my passport, although the piece of paper on which I typed out the eulogy—and which has travelled with me to Africa, China, Paris and back to Africa—has torn so that it's now three pieces of paper.

But I can easily piece the words back together again . . .

Her quiet gift of great common sense; her unerring instinct for knowing when something was wrong—her ability to forgive all; her wisdom, her loyalty, her many talents never boasted of; her wonderful sense of the absurd; an innocence and honesty of spirit that's enchanting.

Not all of my memories are centred around images of Mum outside, or at home, although this is where I 'see' her most, in all her various roles. She was strict about keeping us to an evening routine of piano practice (her own parents had always refused her a piano), and she would wander in and out of the room as we pounded away, humming in tune—or singing aloud when we practised our scales.

I also remember the many occasions when she would stand in the pre-dawn chill at the end of the drive if my father, a doctor, was unusually late getting home after being called out to an emergency in the small hours.

In turn, I would stand at their bedroom window and watch her.

She would stay in the same position for ages until finally his car came down the street. Then I would go back to bed.

We transport our memories . . . Before Mum died, one of my two sisters lived for a couple of years in Singapore, and sometimes I went to stay with her.

Often when I was there—and because I'm a poor sleeper, like my mother—I would walk out onto the balcony on hot, humid nights to breathe the night air. Once, I watched red lightning, the colour of Chinese lanterns, flashing in the sky a long way off towards the east.

Then I would walk into the living room just to see my sister's four ornate Chinese cabinets in the moonlight. The cabinets, in that silvery light, appeared mysterious: keepers of secrets. I would open one and take out my mother's mahjong set, which Mum had insisted my sister keep.

She had taught us—my brothers, sisters and me—to play when we were children. China in those days seemed so remote a country as to be almost imaginary. I found mahjong incredibly exotic. The click-clack of the small, exquisitely painted ivory tiles drifting through the house on Sunday afternoons is another powerful memory.

My sister had suspended four white wire baskets strung with glass crystals, in the shape of ice-cream cones, from the railing of her Singapore apartment. At dusk she would light the tiny red tea lights which she had placed inside the crystals.

The two of us would sit on the balcony talking about my mother, and mahjong, and her love of tea lights. She kept boxes of them in the cupboard in the hall at home. After she died, I found two boxes left. I use them now: but I have to buy more. I cannot use the last few tea lights in the remaining box.

There is something else that happened after my mother died which isn't to do with memory. It's to do with a tragic, terrible event in our family and it's to do with belief in enigmas, those things that can't be explained rationally or scientifically. It's also to do with love, and luminosity.

Three weeks after Mum died, my older brother took his own life.

He didn't commit suicide as a result of my mother's death, and he was the very last person you'd imagine capable of killing himself.

My mother and brother had a complicated relationship. My mother could be very critical of him, but they were very close. Sometimes they would simply look at each other and know what the other was thinking. 'Oh yes, I think so,' one of them would say aloud, with no other words having been spoken. And they'd both nod.

My brother was a lawyer. He had a lawyer's logical way of looking at life. He was pragmatic, with a very dry wit, and not given to displays of affection or emotion. I didn't realise until the last few years before his death that he also had a deep romantic streak. He told me he no longer wanted to practise law, and had decided to become a travel writer. I am certain that his growing desire to write and to travel was real—although looking back at the conversations we had when he pressed me beyond reason and logic to find him a job as a writer *right away*, I see signs that he was already suffering from the depression that would soon overwhelm him.

In fact, it turned out that he'd been behaving in an unpredictable manner for years, but my sister-in-law had courageously kept this hidden from his siblings and parents.

His colleagues never guessed anything was amiss either. He continued to work, to fight and win cases. Socially, he remained jocular, popular, charming.

While we know that our mother's death wasn't the direct cause of our brother's suicide, he started talking about suicide only after her death.

Mum died in hospital just before dawn. We had thought she still had a few days, maybe even another week. My brother was in New Zealand. We rang him immediately but his phone kept ringing out, which it never did—and certainly not during this period with Mum slipping away. We all kept our phones turned on twenty-four hours a day.

Then my siblings and I began receiving SMS messages from him, thanking us for our support and sending us his love. Alarm bells rang. We all hit our phones yet again. His wife was doing the same. Where was he? Where had he gone?! We rang and rang . . . and finally, our brother answered one of the calls.

I think that at some level we realised the significance of those SMS messages when they arrived, but our grief at Mum's death was all consuming and only much, much later did we put all the pieces together and realise that he'd been preparing to kill himself the same morning and more or less at the same time as our mother died. He didn't know, as he was getting ready to take his own life, the first time, that she'd gone.

About a week after Mum's funeral, I had a drink with my brother in the city early one evening. The previous night we'd had dinner together. Like everyone, I was increasingly worried about the despair he was in—he believed that everyone thought him worthless, and he said he *was* worthless—but the idea of him killing himself seemed so far from reality that I simply didn't believe he was capable of it.

We should have realised how close he was to the edge, but we were mourning our mother: we were sometimes even a little impatient in the days following her death as he kept bringing conversations back to himself and the mess he insisted he'd made of his life. We didn't see the tragedy waiting to happen.

'I know, I know,' my brother said at one point that evening, when we were in the bar having a drink, after I'd remarked that suicide was such an alien idea that he couldn't seriously be considering it. 'It's ridiculous,' he agreed with a faint smile, and for a second he was like our old brother again. Sensible, not given to wild remarks, taking everything in his stride.

But then, as we walked back along the street after leaving the bar, I noticed that he was gazing into some strange middle distance, and he looked so lost as we parted—he was staying a few days at my parents' house, with Dad—that before he disappeared into the crowds of people hurrying to go home, I reached up and kissed my undemonstrative brother on the cheek.

'Thank you, darling,' I heard Mum say.

How do you rationalise such a moment? You do not. You believe that it happened, because it did happen. I didn't imagine it. I heard my mother's voice as clearly as if she'd been standing right next to me—so clearly that I turned around in shock.

When I turned back again, my brother was almost invisible in the crowds of pedestrians crossing the street. And that was my last sight of him.

Two weeks later, walking in a dazed state with the rest of my family behind his coffin, out into the cold, blustery late afternoon where still more people, unable to get into the church, were standing dozens deep—and my brother had believed people thought him worthless—I said to myself: 'Thank God Mum didn't live to see this.'

'A mother's job is never finished,' retorted my mother.

Again, I heard her voice as clearly and strongly as before—only this time I wasn't amazed in the slightest. I merely thought, 'Yes, of course. Her job isn't finished. She's with her firstborn, taking care of him.'

In the months following my brother's funeral, I began to contemplate my mother's relationship with him, and his relationship with her, and to remember small incidents and fragments of conversations that made me realise—why had I never realised it before?—that her criticism of him, which often upset the rest of us, in fact camouflaged a fierce protectiveness. She adored him. And probably from the very beginning she sensed the fragility in my brother that the rest of us never saw.

Gradually I began to feel a great sense of comfort and even serenity, and to believe that the timing of their deaths, so close together, was somehow meant to be. And I stopped worrying that it could be a type of madness to entertain such thoughts. My mother wasn't alone. My brother was with her. She had left ahead of him, but he'd caught up with her. Perhaps he had hurried to catch up with her.

So it's curious that only recently did I remember my mother's remarkable intuitiveness, which everyone who knew her had always agreed was out of the ordinary. There were times when it seemed to verge on foreknowledge. Mum's sixth sense.

During the eighteen months when she was back at home after her extended stay in intensive care—and before her health began to decline for the last time—she came out with an unexpected remark one Saturday afternoon while I was spending a couple of hours with her.

'Life will go on, you know,' she said, looking at me intently.

I thought Mum was referring to the time when she would no longer be here, and gently changed the subject.

She shook her head in exasperation. 'Life will go on, Nikki,' she said again.

'Yes, I know, darling,' I answered. 'But let's concentrate on the here and now.'

'I'm talking about *you*,' said my mother, continuing to gaze hard at me. I thought she was simply repeating herself, and I thought no more about it.

Two years after the deaths of my mother and brother, Alain, the Frenchman who had been my partner for over two decades, came home from his usual late-afternoon swim in the ocean unnaturally breathless. He looked scared.

'This isn't normal,' he said.

By five o'clock the next morning he was struggling to breathe. By six am he was in intensive care.

Seven weeks later, he was dead.

A rare, aggressive form of lung cancer had come, it seemed, from nowhere. His specialists, mystified by some of the scans in the first month of his illness, hedged when it came to a diagnosis—while I pushed from my mind something that Alain had been saying to me for some time.

'I get the feeling that I don't have much time left.'

Nor did I remember what my mother had said.

Life changed horribly, irrevocably. Alain didn't stay long in intensive care, but it was only the first crisis. He spent the next few weeks in and out of hospital, always desperate to get home again.

He died very suddenly, shortly before eight o'clock one Tuesday morning. Even before that moment, everything had stopped seeming real. The absence of reality would soon be followed by the reality of absence—and in time reality itself, as I had known it in my 'previous' life, became a distant memory.

A week after his funeral, the phone rang in our house.

I'd lost all track of time; I think the call came shortly before noon. One of his cancer specialists was on the other end of the line, a woman who could be brusque, and she sounded politely cross.

'They said Alain didn't show at chemo today. Is everything all right? Where is he?' she asked.

It took me a few seconds to answer.

'He died,' I replied.

There was, not unexpectedly, total silence at the other end of the line.

When my caller started speaking again the whole tenor of her voice had changed. She'd been away overseas at a conference, she explained, and had only just returned. This didn't explain why no one in the chemotherapy department seemed to know about Alain's death, but I was beyond caring about hospitals' poor interdepartmental communication.

The two of us went on to talk for a considerable amount of time, and eventually I told her something that ordinarily I would have baulked at saying to a scientist.

Perhaps I should have prefaced what I told her by explaining that Alain used to cook leek soup for my mother as she became increasingly frail, always insisting that leek soup— although only French leek soup, and his grandmother's recipe in particular—was the cure for all ills. Instead, I went straight to an incident that had taken place twenty-four hours before he died.

At some stage during that last weekend at home, Alain lost all his strength and could no longer sit up in bed without help. By Sunday night he had stopped speaking altogether. I assumed that this was due to the toxic effects of his second bout of chemo, on the Thursday before, although at some level, I felt terror.

At eight o'clock on Monday morning, he suddenly pushed himself up against the pillows I'd heaped around him and said in a strong, matter-of-fact voice, 'Your mum is here.'

I heard my voice speaking from some place in the distance, or so it seemed. There was an echo in my ears.

'Is she?'

'Yes!' exclaimed Alain, and he actually sounded irritated. 'Can't you see her?'

He remained half sitting up for a few moments more, then lay back on the pillows and closed his eyes.

And so, I said to Alain's doctor on the phone, commenting as well that I realised how this sounded, I believed that the only logical explanation for Alain's sudden death was that my mother came and got him to end his suffering, and mine.

There was another silence at the end of the phone. I assumed she was trying to work out what to say and how best to say it sympathetically without disavowing rational thought; she would probably talk gently about the medication he'd been on, and the possible hallucinogenic effects.

'I imagine that someone like you would laugh at what I've just said,' I added.

There came the reply that I've never forgotten, and not least because of the absolute sincerity with which she spoke.

'You know,' said this formidable cancer specialist, who would have seen so many deaths, and perhaps had lost her mother too, 'the longer I do this job, the less sure I am about anything.'

Dedicated to my father Ian, my sisters Anne and Prue, and my surviving brother Paul.

DREAMS OF HER REAL SELF

HELEN GARNER

IT WAS ALWAYS CLEAR TO me what would happen when my parents died.

Dad would pitch forward without warning into the grave he had dug with his knife and fork. The struggle that had shaped and distorted my character would be over. I would be elated to see the back of him. Then I would torture myself with guilt for the rest of my life.

Free of his domineering presence, my mother would creep out from under her stone. She would show herself at last. At last I would know her. Shyly she would befriend her five remaining children, maybe even come to live with one of us. She would take up her golf clubs again, pull on her flowery bathing cap and swim in the surf, simmer her modest vegetable soups, knit cardigans in quiet stripes with a lot of grey. In a few years she would fade, weaken and slip away. Surely, about her, I would feel only a mild sorrow that would pass in the manner that nature intended.

She went first.

In her early eighties Dad dragged her to the last of the scores of dwellings he had imposed on her during their long marriage, a seventh-floor apartment in central Melbourne that in a fit of Schadenfreude he had bought from a member of her family whose finances had hit the wall. Isolated up there, with a view of St Patrick's cathedral and Parliament House, she sank into a stunned, resentful gloom shot through with flashes of bitter sarcasm. She would point at a gin and tonic on the table and say, in a grim, warning tone, 'Mark my words. In a minute that ice is going to melt. Then the glass will overflow, and there'll be a *hell* of a mess to clean up.' She slumped into depression, then drifted away into dementia. She wandered at night. She fell and fractured a bone. Her body withered. In a nursing home she became savage, bestial. She snarled at us and lashed out with her claws. Lost to herself and to us, she died at last, by means of something I can only call chemical mercy. My youngest sister and I, strained and silent, chanced to be the only ones at her bedside when she exhaled her last hoarse breath.

People we had hardly seen since childhood, friends she had left behind in obedience to Dad's driven restlessness, came to her funeral. They spoke of her with tender faces.

After she died, we persuaded our father to sell his flat and buy the shabby little house next door to me. He was too proud to be looked after and he didn't like my cooking. But for two years he flourished. He zoomed to the neighbourhood cafes on a motorised scooter. He came to hear a blues band at the Elwood RSL. He began to keep company with a woman he had fancied before he married Mum, a stylish widow from Geelong who was not afraid to take it right up to him. He had to ask his daughters for advice on his love-life. He liked a spontaneous drive to the country to look at the crops. In the car we were always laughing.

One scorching summer morning, at breakfast time, he told me he hadn't been able to get his breath in the shower. I buckled his sandals onto him and called an ambulance. On Hoddle Street his heart stopped. The paramedics got it going and swept into St Vincent's emergency. The family rushed in. He was ninety-one: the doctors decided to take him off the ventilator. We stood around him in a tearful circle. They whisked out the tube. He took a huge shuddering gasp, and began to breathe strongly. The doctors and nurses joined in our shout of laughter. The stubborn old bull would never die. He was admitted to a private room on the seventh floor. That evening the others went down to the street for a meal and I stayed with him. He was unconscious, breathing without help in a steady rhythm. A nurse came in to check on him. While she bent over him to smooth the sheet under his chin, I moved away from the bed and turned to look out the window of the high, west-facing room. The sun was going down in a blaze over the Exhibition Gardens. He breathed in. He breathed out. He was silent. I said, 'He's gone.' The nurse, surprised, felt for his pulse. 'Yes. He's gone.' She left the room. I blessed him. I sat with him quietly for ten minutes, on a chair near the window. Then I started texting the others to come back.

My father's mother died, in Hopetoun, when he was two. He had a sternly loving stepmother, but there was always something of the abandoned child about him. He was as entitled and as quick to anger as a toddler. He was jealous, impatient, rivalrous, scornful, suspicious. He could not trust anyone. He could not keep friends; by the end of his life, he had none. He was middle class, a wool merchant, with money but no education. He never read a book. One of my husbands, put through Dad's insulting third degree about whether he was 'living off' me, said he was a peasant. Yet with strangers he had great charm. 'I thank you, sir, from the bottom of my heart.' He had an unerring ear for music, though he never sang except ironically. He was a good ballroom dancer. He could shape a story. He liked to laugh. 'I've never *seen* such a deflated manager.' On Mum's headstone it seemed right to mention the word *love*. For his, we could not find a short phrase to encapsulate his contradictions, our exhausting struggles. We ended up with *Our father, a boy from the Mallee*. People who had not known him were startled by the bluntness of the epitaph. But to me, at least, it evokes a landscape of complex meaning, forlorn, sometimes beautiful: a desert that now and then bloomed.

I set out to write about my mother, but already I am talking about my father.

He is easy to write about. He was a vivid, obstreperous character whose jolting behaviour was a spectacle, an endurance test that united his children in opposition to him. Things he did or failed to do gave rise to hundreds of stories that we still share and embellish.

To write about her at length, coherently, is almost beyond me. He blocked my view of her, as he blocked her horizon. I can think about her only at oblique angles and in brief bursts, in no particular order.

When my daughter was a teenager she had a dog, a poodle-cross called Polly. Polly fell down the crack between two of my marriages. She trudged again and again across inner Melbourne to my ex-husband's house, and died a lonely painful death, by misadventure, in a suburban backyard. She was an anxious creature, timid and appeasing, who provoked in me an overwhelming impatience. She would lie at my feet, tilting her head on this angle and that, striving for eye contact. The more she begged for it, the less I could give.

In just such a way, over many years, I refused my mother eye contact. She longed for it. I withheld it. I lacerate myself with this memory, with the connection I can't expunge between lost mother and lost dog.

When, in the street, I see a mother walking with her grown-up daughter, I can hardly bear to witness the mother's pride, the softening of her face, her incredulous joy at being granted her daughter's company; and the iron discipline she imposes on herself, to muffle and conceal this joy.

Elizabeth Jolley wrote that 'the strong feeling of love which goes from the parent to the child does not seem part of the child which can be given back to the parent'. But last spring, at a big and brilliant community show to celebrate the reopening of Melbourne's concert hall, a clever conductor divided the audience and taught us to sing in parts. A thousand euphoric strangers sang, in time and in tune, a slow-modulating melody. In the row in front of me sat an old woman and her daughter. Too absorbed in singing even to glance at each other, they reached, they gripped hands, they did not let go until the song was done.

A few years before she entered her final decline, my mother and I went together to hear a famous string trio. We arrived early, took our front-row seats high in the gallery, and looked down at the stage. It was bare, except for three chairs. My mother said, 'Looks a bit sad, doesn't it.' Surprised, as if at a witticism, I swung to face her. She raised her eyebrows and grinned at me. We both began to laugh. I was filled with respect. Whenever I remember that moment, the hopeless thing in my heart stops aching, and finds a small place to stand.

I came home from university armed with the Baroque. Bach and Vivaldi, their stringent impersonality, made my mother's favourite records sound overemotional and corny. Now, if I turn on the car radio and hear Tchaikovsky or Brahms, I find tears running down my cheeks. Perhaps that's where I can find her, take her hand and walk with her: across the fields and through the splendid forests of the Romantic piano concertos she loved.

She was not confident, or quick. She did not sense the right moment to speak. She did not know how to gain and hold attention. When she told a story, she felt a need to establish enormous quantities of irrelevant background information. She took so long to get to the point that her listeners would tune out and start talking about something else. Family shorthand for this, behind her back, was 'And then I breathed.'

Shows of affection were not done in our family. We could not even hug without an ironic shoulder pat. Expressions of emotion were frowned upon. 'You great cake. Pick up your lip before you trip over it.' I saw her, as an old woman, have to muster the courage to hold out her arms for someone else's baby. Perhaps this is why she never knew that her grandchildren were fond of her. She was shy with them. Once she said to me, in her timid, patient way, 'I don't think they like me much.'

Only last week, though, there floated into my awareness, from a cache of treasures Dad had left behind, a passionately misspelt little tribute that their nine-year-old granddaughter, my niece, had written when Mum was dying. It is accompanied by a drawing: a roast chicken on a rug and far in the background two figures, one large and one small, walking away hand in hand. 'Me, Grandpa and her went on picnics in the sun, just near her house in Kew. The sun was bright and the food was delicious, mostly chicken and potatoes and sometimes delicious sandwiches. Then we would go back home and read or watch telly. But what I liked was often we would go into her room and look in the cupboards and see all theese speicial things of hers some belonging to her six children one of which is my mum. I love all six of them and give them my best dreams of Grandma, dreams of her real self, the self with no evil diaseases, the strongest part of her body and everyone should know its still here.'

I think my mother was afraid of me. I went to university, the first of her children to move beyond her ability to contain, or help. In 1972 I was fired from the Education Department for answering my students' questions about sex. There were cartoons for and against me in the newspapers. She showed me a letter of protest she had laboriously written to the editor of the *Age*. The letter revealed that she had not understood the irony of the cartoons. The one she most hated was the one that most strongly defended me. I tried to explain this gently, but I knew she was humiliated.

I was the eldest of six children. They kept coming. I must have been taught to change a nappy, fill a bottle, wheel a pram, rock an infant to sleep. Yet I cannot remember there ever being a baby in the house.

~

The clean, modest architecture of Victorian baby health centres has always comforted me.

When my daughter was born, I was estranged from my father. He had tried to prevent me from marrying my first husband, thus mortally offending his decent and generous parents. My mother had defied him and come to our wedding, at which one bottle of champagne sufficed for the entire company. But at the time of our baby's birth she was unable to break through his veto. She did not come to the hospital. I don't remember hoping that she would, or being upset that she didn't. Years later my youngest sister told me she recalled, as a very small girl, sitting in the car outside my house with our father, waiting for Mum to come out. So she must have fought her way past him. I have no memory of her visit.

Towards the end of Mum's life, when she was already becoming vague and fearful but was not yet demented, my widowed sister Marie was often angry with her, scornful and harsh in a way that made me flinch. The grief of her widowhood had stirred up some old rage in her that I did not understand. One day Mum asked my sister to drive her down to the Mornington Peninsula, to visit our aunt. She obliged. Next time I saw Mum, she told me, without complaint and in a puzzled tone, that when my sister had delivered her home after that outing, she had brusquely put her hand out for petrol money.

Last year I went to the Australian War Memorial in

Canberra. I had expected dusty old weapons and dioramas of heroism. Instead, I found a curatorial work of inspired brilliance and grandeur, and a chapter of my mother's life that I had never before bothered to fit into the history of the twentieth century. At the desk I told the attendant the name of my uncle Noel, Mum's favourite younger brother, who was killed in the Second World War. To us she rarely spoke of him. Dad, a wool trader, was in a reserved occupation; was the war a touchy subject? But when Dad was very old, he told me that Mum had been devastated by her brother's death. She never got over it; he was 'like her twin'.

The man at the war museum turned to a computer, pressed a few keys, and handed me two sheets of paper. Flight-Sergeant. Aerial Gunner RAAF. Cause of death: Flying Battle. Lancaster crashed at Hollenstein, Germany, while returning from a raid over Brunswick on 12–13 August 1944, killing all crew members. At last I registered the dates. I had to sit down. He must have been barely twenty. When my mother got the news that his plane had crashed, I would have been a toddler of eighteen months, and my sister an infant, five weeks old. How could she have mothered us, staggering under such a blow? In her old age Mum said to me, 'Marie was a very thin and *hungry* baby—always crying and wanting more.'

Once, while my mother was staying a weekend with me, a man I was having an affair with came to see me. He behaved sweetly towards her, questioned her about her life. He asked about her childhood and her family. How had the news of her brother's death in the war come to her: by phone, or was there a letter? She seemed astonished that someone should be interested in her. When he left, she turned to me and said, '*He's* nice.' 'He's the love of my life, Mum,' I burst out, shocking myself, 'but he's married.' I suppose I thought she would disapprove. But she cried, 'Oh!' She leapt off her chair and threw her arms around me. She said, 'Just wait.'

From what life experience, from what instinct she drew this spontaneous advice I have no idea.

She got on well with all the men in my life, and they liked her. She continued to have warm feelings for them, and they for her, years after they and I had wrecked everything and gone our separate ways.

For my work, on tram stops, in planes, in courts, I'm not afraid to question any stranger. But I never sat my mother down and pressed her about the past, about her life before me, before our father.

One evening she and Dad and I came out of a restaurant. The street was empty of traffic for a mile in each direction. I stepped confidently off the kerb but she seized the tail of my jacket and pulled me back. 'We'll cross at the lights. I'm a very. Law-abiding. Person.'

My mother was good at sewing. When I was five or so she made me a pair of pyjamas on her Singer machine. I refused to wear them because they had frills on the bottom. She pleaded with me. She told me that if I wore the pyjamas, fairies would come and they would like me because of the frills. I did not care about the fairies. Even at that age I sensed the guilty power my refusal gave me.

It seemed to me, as a child, that our mother was hopeless at giving birthday parties. The cakes she made weren't right. The decorations and games somehow missed the mark. Other kids' mothers knew how to do a party right but Mum didn't. Instead of her plain cupcakes with icing, I secretly thought, she should have made those cakes with whipped cream and little tilted wings on top that other girls' mothers presented. It was a very strong sense I had, that there was something she did not get. All my adult life I despised myself for my disloyalty. It did not comfort me to learn that all children felt their mothers to be socially lacking in some crucial way. But one day when she was old and we were talking about motherhood, she said with a casual little laugh, 'I was never any good at giving kids' parties. I somehow never had the knack.'

She used to wear hats that pained me. Shy little round beige felt hats with narrow brims. Perhaps one was green. And she stood with her feet close together, in sensible shoes.

Oh, if only she would walk in here now.

She must have been only in her late thirties when she developed a gum disease and had to have all her teeth extracted. If she had gone to a Melbourne dentist, instead of remaining loyal to the doddery old fellow who treated our family in Geelong, a less drastic treatment might have been found. Not only did he pull out all her teeth, he whacked the false ones in over her bleeding gums. She came home and sat by the fire, hunched in her dressing gown, eyes down, holding a hanky to her mouth. We did not know how to comfort her. We tiptoed around her, whispering, going about our business. Thirty years later, at home on my own one night, I saw on SBS a movie called *Germany, Pale Mother* in which a woman in wartime had all her teeth removed as a cure for her neurasthenic state. I sat breathless on the couch while the dentist in his white coat yanked out her teeth and dropped them one by one with a clang into a metal dish.

My sax-playing sister, a professional, came over last winter with her ukulele and a Johnny Cash CD. She sings in the eighty-voice Melbourne Mass Gospel Choir, but is highly sceptical of all things religious. She wanted me to listen to 'Wayfaring Stranger'. All I knew was that it is an old song of weariness, of sin; of the longing to cross over Jordan.

'Come on,' she said. 'It's only got a couple of chords. We can learn it in five minutes.'

I got my uke down off the shelf. We tuned up. Yes, it was easy, the music part.

'Listen to that harmonium-playing,' she said. 'It's exemplary.'

But the lyrics.

I know dark clouds will gather round me,
I know my way is hard and steep.
But beauteous fields arise before me,
Where God's redeemed their vigils keep.
I'm going there to see my mother.
She said she'd meet me when I come.
I'm just going over Jordan.
I'm just going over home.

I said nothing, just worked at getting the strum right. That night, after she'd left, I played along with Johnny Cash for a long time. I could hardly get the words out, but his voice, weary and cracked, gave the song a majesty that still welcomed the humble chords of a ukulele.

My mother was a natural athlete: neat, small and graceful. I was hopeless at sport of any kind. All I wanted to do was read and write. At fourteen I got my first typewriter, my grandmother's reconditioned Smith Corona portable. Mum asked me to type out the results of the Point Lonsdale Golf Club ladies' tournament, to be reported in the *Geelong Advertiser*. Perhaps she was trying to interest me in what she cared about, or was simply looking for something we could do together. At the time I took it at face value: my first typing job. We toiled together at the kitchen table after tea. She dictated, and I clattered away at my beautiful oil-scented machine, on the quarto paper of which we had bought a ream at Griffiths Bookstore. She did not lose her temper at my mistakes. I felt important and useful. We were pleased with each other when the job was done. Two mornings later we stood shoulder to shoulder, looking down proudly at the newspaper's inky columns.

I must have been about twelve when the insight came to me that my mother's entire life was divided into compartments. None of them was any longer than the number of hours between one meal and the next. She was on a short leash. I don't recall thinking that this would be *my* fate, or resolving to avoid it. All I remember is the picture of her life, and the speechless desolation that filled me.

Mrs Thatcher has told one of her interviewers that she had nothing to say to her mother after she reached the age of fifteen. Such a sad, blunt confession it seems, and yet not a few of us could make it. The world moves on so fast, and we lose all chance of being the women our mothers were; we lose all understanding of what shaped them.

Hilary Mantel

The quietly mighty Japanese film director Yasujiro Ozu tells story after story of adult children breaking away from their parents. His characters rarely cry or raise their voices. Their emotions are expressed in tiny signs and changes of position. A father looks down at his glass. A mother folds her hands, or draws a handkerchief from her sleeve. These subtle movements call up in me surges of excruciating sympathy for my parents, for the hurt, helpless, angry love they must have felt as they watched me smash my way out of their protection.

In Dad's house I found a little photo of him and Mum in their twenties, sitting on the front step of their first house. Between them lay a long-eared black dog, a spaniel. Dad said his name was Ned. I did not remember our ever having had a pet. I asked if the dog had died before I was born. 'Ah no. I had to get rid of him. Mum wouldn't let him inside. Because of her *brand-new mushroom-pink carpet.*' He laughed, and shrugged. 'I put an ad in the paper. A lady came round and took him. She tied his lead to the carrier of her bike and pedalled away. I thought he might have looked back, but he never even turned his head.'

A crime novelist spoke at a conference about the unsuitability of his usual sardonic tone for the war story he was trying to write, 'about young men with their stomachs torn open who cry all night for their mothers and then die'. An old man told me, after he had had open-heart surgery, that he and a whole ward full of other men his age woke in the dark from hideous nightmares, screaming for their mothers. I have never read or heard of a woman in extremis who called for her mother. It is not possible for me to imagine such a thing. Still, I did hear about a woman of my age who had died in a distant part of the country. Her parents did not go to her funeral. Shocked by this, I asked my mother, 'Would you go to my funeral, if I died far away?' She uttered a sharp pant of disbelief. 'If you died in the Arctic *Circle* I'd make m' way there.'

On my pantry shelf stands a tall storage jar that I salvaged from Dad's kitchen when we sold his house. It survived the successive demolitions of my mother's households and, I suspect, of her mind. She has labelled it, in her large, clear hand: *Sultanas*. Then she has crossed out *Sultanas* and replaced it with *Currants*. Then she has crossed out *Currants* and restored *Sultanas*. The jar, when I found it, was empty.

Her ghost is in my body. I have her long narrow feet with low arches. I have her hollow bones, her hysterectomy, her fading eyebrows, her fine grey-brown hair that resists all attempts at drama. My movements are hers when, on a summer morning, I close up the house against the coming scorcher, or in the evening whisk the dry clothes off the line in weightless armfuls that conceal my face.

In the intermission at *Shane Warne: The Musical* two smiling strangers approached me. The man introduced himself and his wife. Aside from our parents' funerals, I had not seen him since we were children.

'I knew you straight away,' he said, 'from the other side of the room. You stand exactly like your mother.'

～

In my forties, when I lived in Chippendale, I used to walk to work across the big gardens of Sydney University. I walked fast, thinking my thoughts. One morning a young woman passed me, going the other way. She was wearing an op shop blouse from the 1940s, striped, with shoulder pads and tiny pearl buttons. At the sight of it a bolt of ecstasy went through me, an atavistic bliss so powerful that its roots could only have been in early childhood. I wrote my mother a letter. Did she ever have a stripy blouse, rather floppy, when I was little?

A week later came a curly-edged black-and-white photo. The date pencilled on the back was 1943. A woman in her early twenties stands in a bare backyard, squinting in an unposed way that raises her cheeks and bares her teeth. Her hair is permed and pinned in a Victory Roll. On her flexed left arm sits a wide-browed, unsmiling baby. The child's right cheek and left hand lean against the stripes of the woman's rayon blouse.

The war is not yet over. Her brother is alive. I am six months old. I am still an only child. She is carrying me in her arms. She is strong enough to bear my weight with ease. I trust her. She is my mother, and I am content to rest my head upon her breast.

THE PASSAGE

JAYA SAVIGE

Weep, child
As you see your mother weep . . .
Seneca *The Trojan Women*

THE SMALL ROUGH STONE WILL not be skimmed. Even when thrown artfully, it catches the water's surface and submerges, before bobbing back up as if for air. Riddled with tiny vesicles, where bubbles of gas were trapped in the suddenly cooled lava, it is lightweight, porous and abrasive: the rock that floats. The ancient Egyptians, who Herodotus tells us only tolerated bodily hair during periods of mourning, used it to depilate and, perhaps more importantly, to polish the fibrous pith of papyrus in preparation for the scribe. When papyrus gave way to sturdier, animal-skin parchment, the rock doubled as an eraser, enabling medieval writers to sand back the ancient vellum, giving us the palimpsest, or 'twice prepared' manuscript of scrubbed text whose trace remains visible (the sole means of survival for some ancient

---

works). Of course, in the age of the word processor, whose delete key rather terrifyingly leaves *no* discernible trace, this usage is obsolete; yet the rock is still used for exfoliating the skin, and for removing ink stains from the fingers of those who persist with older methods. It has a more recent use too: as part of a compound for acoustic tiling, to soundproof rooms for music practice.

In summer the sand islands in Moreton Bay, of which this is the northernmost, bask in a subtropical lassitude. Dune grasses bend in the coastal breeze, the tide pushes its barrow. The stretch of water separating us from the mainland is the Pumicestone Passage, which speculates its way north towards the Sunshine Coast through a shifting maze of salt-marsh islets and sandy shoals. In the final days of 2001, I find myself returning here, to Banksia Beach, on the calm side. The majestic Glasshouse Mountains loom on the western horizon, a cluster of massive trachyte cores, remnants of an ancient family of volcanoes. Behind me rises a set of fibreglass replicas, to scale, of the three major peaks: the brooding, heavy-shouldered father, Tibrogargan; Beerwah, the capacious mother; and the delinquent child, Coonowrin, or 'Crookneck', eldest of eight, with his broken neck. Every child schooled in the Caboolture Shire knows the indigenous Dreamtime story that tells how Tibrogargan belted the young Coonowrin for neglecting his pregnant mother, Beerwah, during the great flood; domestic violence, it seems, was not only a trope of Greek mythology. As a child I scaled the miniature replicas in a deluge of peach and magenta at sunset, as my young siblings do now.

I have come here to forget. Or is it to remember? Perhaps the two are indistinguishable. To forget, certainly, my mum's incomprehensible suffering; her face, sucked to a pitiful husk at forty-two, as though by a golden orb spider, after months cocooned in death's web, feeding it. Yes, death grew fat on my mum. Ravaged to within a kiss of recognition by a one-way journey through a nightmarish wilderness of morphine, the dose rising as inexorably as the tide, until the twin darknesses of sleep and death finally washed over. I am here to erase *this* memory, so that I might remember her instead in life, vivacious, high-spirited. But I am naive. The pumice will not do. The waters of the passage will not do. Only the slow rub of years might one day smooth away the imprint left by her suffering, her heaving up of each final breath, almost a minute apart, as I clutched her skeletal hand. Across the bed, my stepfather, whom I've called 'Dad' since the age of seven, wrecked with exhaustion. The last, rasping exhalation, which will accompany me until my own.

Here, where the shore meets the scrub, is a host of respiratory tubers piping up through the sand like rubbery snorkels, the breathing apparatus of a stolid grey mangrove—my sanctuary this overcast morning. I try to block out the oxygen mask, and my pathetic attempt to feed her her favourite ice-cream, the stupid mess. With the sodden digits squishing beneath my feet, I come to admire this tree's endeavour and perhaps even envy its success. Committed, more permanent than the knots of spotted mangroves further up the passage, with their stilted roots loosened. For all its seeming resignation, this grey has cheated the limits of its occasion: soaked in salt, it has discovered a way to resurface and to breathe.

∿

All the pumice in the passage could not have soundproofed the beach to my brother's unholy squeal the day he decided to help a dehydrated stingray, victim of the swift ebb tide, back into its element. As recent migrants from the cold south, and from an earlier life I am only just beginning to piece together, we had arrived unschooled in the perils of the shore, unlike my soon-to-be cousins, who could pick up crabs by their back legs before they could talk. Their fathers, seasoned trawlermen, speak soberly of the excruciating pain of the stingray barb, said to occupy the rung of agony below only the deadly stonefish. At the time of his encounter with that gasping prehistoric creature, my brother was four years old.

I was six, a little way along the beach, and turned instantly. It seemed at first that he had been bitten by madness. His little chicken-legs were already blurring with an urgency that would've been comic, were it not for the ear-splitting accompaniment. I spot an approaching sedan. The strange ability memory has of slowing down time in recollection of intense experiences allows me to identify this moment as my earliest experience of fear for a life; the sickening knowledge that nothing will alter the course of his sprint across the beachfront road; the relief in seeing him make it, hearing the car brakes squeal in poor imitation of his own. It was then that I realised my brother was not impelled by a madness at all, but by a kind of inexorable logic. Whatever the nature of his terrible question, the answer was our mother, not a hundred metres away at our friends' beachfront weatherboard. He was not flapping about, as I first thought, like a loose tarpaulin in a storm. No, he was a spring-loaded retractable wire, whizzing back viciously to his source.

❧

Several times during the night before my mother died, her ragged breath snagged on the imminent dark as she stirred in panic. 'Agitated' had been the nurse's word, said warmly enough as she upped the merciful poppy yet again. But the word did not sound right. When I hear the word 'agitated', I think of a spectrum of behaviour ranging perhaps from that of a parent hearing of an accident at school camp, to someone who just can't sit still. Maybe that was it; my mum wouldn't lie still for death. And she didn't, either. She was a fighter; everyone knew where my mum stood, from school to church, supermarket to beach. Having had me at nineteen in Sydney, my brother two years later, then moving as a single mother of two half-Indonesian children to an island in Queensland, had honed her flinty maternal intelligence to something remarkable. My mother wasn't 'agitated'; she was Prometheus, cursed to have her organs pecked each day by a razor-beaked crow, only they weren't growing back.

But who was I to hold the poor nurse to account for the terrifying inadequacy of language? Besides, I had heard the pure, spare lyrics my mum had mouthed as she started from death's embrace during that unforgettable night: my younger siblings' names. I could tell by the syllables. The labour of each utterance made it almost as though she were giving birth to each of us again: my four youngest siblings to our new dad, an earthy tradesman with an eye for timber; then my brother, and finally myself. And as her son, I knew what she was doing: *she* was grieving for *us*. That the high-tensile wire of blood connecting a mother to her children would be severed prematurely, with no source to spring back to, just as it was most needed for the twins, both ten, my brother of eleven and sister of thirteen. When the nurse touched my wrist, saying gently, 'I think it's time,' I rose to the edge and felt as if I were plummeting from a wall, unable to grip the spinning earth. It was her, grieving for us.

⁓

Astyanax was a boy at the time of the Trojan War. He was thrown from the walls of Troy to his death by the victorious Greeks, to prevent him avenging his father, the great warrior and crown prince Hector, firstborn to King Priam and Queen Hecuba. His death receives a passing mention in Homer's *Iliad*, Virgil's *Aeneid* and Ovid's *Metamorphoses*. The mourning of his mother, Andromache, and paternal grandmother, the widowed Queen Hecuba and others, are the subject of Euripides' *The Women of Troy*, which to my mind approximates the wailing of mothers, wives and daughters we see on the news from Syria or the West Bank. But it is only in Seneca's version of the story that young Astyanax's separation from his mother is dramatised. Seneca even gives the boy two rare words, his only utterance in the classical sources mentioned—*'Miserere, mater'* ('Have mercy, mother!', sometimes translated as 'No! Mother!')—spoken in the 'few more moments' grace' granted by the impatient Greek warrior Ulysses, before the boy is ripped from his mother's bosom. Later, a messenger relates the boy's death to his mother in grotesque detail: 'From that sheer fall / What body can remain? [. . .]/ The brains spilled from the shattered skull. He lies / a shapeless corpse.'

This scene of the separation of the boy Astyanax from his mother became a cipher for my own loss in the years following my mother's death. There is evidence for this in one of several poems concerning my grief that appear in my first book, *Latecomers*, which is dedicated to her. It begins:

> In hindsight her backache
> Was the suffering of Andromache.
>
> Dawn bludgeons its hegemonic pax.
> I over-balance, an everyday Astyanax

With the distance of a decade, I realise now what should have been obvious at the time: that in conscripting the story of Astyanax's tragic separation from his mother, I was in fact reversing the roles. For in the Greek myth, it is of course the *son* who dies, leaving the mother, Andromache, to mourn *him*— precisely the opposite of my own experience. Of course, Greek mythology—like pop music, so devastating in its banality, for grievers and jilted lovers alike—is nothing if not a narrative prism through which people have refracted the searching, sometimes sputtering light of their own personalities. Yet there is also a kind of epistemological panic to be endured by a poet who feels acutely the discrepancy between cold matters of fact and the slippery, metaphorical nature of language; the very reason Plato would have poets banished from his ideal state. Thankfully, the poetic impulse sometimes turns out to have been a step ahead of the rational mind, and this, I think, was one such example. For my conscription of the Greek myth was not primarily, it seems clear to me, to identify myself with Astyanax, but to come to a deeper understanding of my mother's own loss—which I could only liken to Andromache's, whose grief is bottomless.

～

My mum knew for years that she was not well, but had not been believed. Eighteen months before she died she was given paracetamol and told to rest; she had been experiencing debilitating pain in her lower back for much of her last five years. Too late they diagnosed it, and in a rearguard move chose to operate, but it had metastasised beyond abeyance. This left her unable to recover from the surgery in time to undergo chemotherapy. It occurred to me that there must have been many women throughout history who had not been believed when telling the story of their bodies to men. I had some idea, from reading Caryl Churchill's *Vinegar Tom*, that this refusal to believe a woman's knowledge of her body had a long history, stemming back at least to the witch trials of the seventeenth century—the Western medical profession having defined itself in opposition to witchcraft, which could include healing—and before that to the Greek concept of *hysteria*, or the travelling womb, deemed the bête noire behind most female ailments. Misogyny was at the heart of Western medicine, I concluded with youthful conviction. There was a name for this affliction: the Cassandra Complex, after the priestess of Troy (and Astyanax's aunt) who foresaw the fall of her city to the Greeks, but was cursed so as not to be believed.

My general animus for doctors, which would last for years, was also due in part to the very real possibility, as I saw it then, that an accurate diagnosis (let alone a successful operation) might depend on whether a doctor's personal life was or wasn't going haywire. Negligence, according to the results of a newspaper competition to redefine familiar English words, might be a woman answering the door in her underwear. I later realised that what I thought I hated about doctors, rather unfairly, was that they were human. I've also accepted that pancreatic cancer remains very difficult to detect, and is one of the few cancers not to have been alleviated in any real way by scientific advancements of recent decades. Worse, however, was the suspicion, much later, that I too may've been complicit in the Cassandra Complex; that I too may have participated in this disbelief, and passed it off romantically as my denial. For denial is forgivable, unlike disbelief.

~

It is a minor triumph of humanity that sees even the most redoubtable atheist invoke the afterlife, out of sheer empathy, to comfort a grieving friend: 'I know she'd be looking out for you.' Perhaps the subjunctive mood suggests here, rather: 'She *would* be looking out for you, *if* you believe that stuff.' And it is surely at least as remarkable when one who considers himself an atheist condescends to prayer; which is what I did, for almost two years, beginning in the months before my mum died. Admittedly, every prayer began in the fashion of Pascal's wager, with an 'If (you are there . . .)'.

I say this as someone who, at the age of twenty-three, referred to Nietszche (not that I'm proud to admit it) in my mother's eulogy. To be fair, as an unsubtle dig at the church it was in a way after her own heart, and I said much else besides. All the same, it happened. 'Nietzsche had foreseen a time,' I said, casting him, I realise now, as an alternative prophet, 'when people had to choose how to act in the knowledge that God was dead. My mother was of this time, and taught us how to think of something spiritually larger than ourselves, in a non-theistic way ...' I can only imagine how mortified Sister Veronica and Sister Hilda must have felt as, through my mother's death tract, I attempted to smuggle revolution into the tiny Orthodox church I'd sung in as a child—though this was probably partly the point.

And yet, in spite of German philosophy, in spite of the Camus-cool of indifference to dying mothers, or Stephen Dedalus' refusal to kneel before his, still I prayed. Simply that she might be taken care of. Even as I did so each night in my rented flat over at the surfside, in Woorim, where I'd moved to be closer to Dad and my younger siblings, I knew that my addressee was a projection; that prayer had for centuries been an institutionalised excuse to talk to oneself, providing absolution from insanity on a technicality. Kierkegaard suggested that faith is precisely belief without reason; but this was prayer without faith. Embracing the contradiction, I felt I had a right to my strange form of secular prayer, my moments of faithless religiosity. I guess I was having my cake and eating it; I could not have been the first. It was around this time that I wrote 'Intercession', which would become the final poem in *Latecomers*. The poem contains what I consider to be the single hardest-won line in the book, forged in those months and years of grief, tempered with sporadic, passionate and earnest Pascalian entreaty: 'Prayer remains the cheapest psychoanalysis.' And still I prayed.

~

Occasionally we borrow one of our uncles' dinghies, a twelve-footer with an eight-horsepower outboard. One summer we cut across the crests to Gilligan's, a large sandbar several hundred metres off the south-western tip of the island, Skirmish Point, where the passage meets the bay proper. Gilligan's surfaces only on the lowest of ebb tides, and is hazardous enough to be marked by a cardinal buoy.

It has taken me the best part of twenty minutes to reel her in, to break her will, the rod bending until I thought it would snap, my adolescent arms aching. But when Dad lifts the thing into the boat, I don't even recognise it: part flathead, part ray, part fish, some evolutionary throwback. 'Shovelnose shark,' he says. The wave of pride that engulfs me on hearing that second word makes me oblivious to the reasons he gives for why we should release it: first, that it is on the small side, at seventy or eighty centimetres; second, there is virtually no chance that we will be eating it; third, it is female. But I am adamant. There is no way I am returning to Uncle Greg's without it. I insist, tyrannically, on my trophy, my proof.

Scooting back up the passage towards the canal at Banksia, the salt spray stinging our faces, I peer into the bucket. Upside down and bent in a semicircle around the inside edge so as to fit on top of several whiting in a couple of inches of water, lies the shovelnose shark. Its gasping has become intermittent; like some slow-motion origami fortune teller, its gills flare open and shut once or twice a minute. Its slimy belly, exposed to the air, begins to twitch, then palpitate, as I notice something start to protrude from the slit near the base of its tail. I thought it was shitting. A sudden gush as a sandy bloody stream jets out over the rest of the fish in the bucket.

Wriggling in the light ochre fluid are the distinct shapes of two miniature shovelnoses, each smaller than my little finger and almost entirely translucent. I can see right through to their spines. Only their eyes are opaque, two minuscule black dots each no larger than a grain of sugar. At first they nose about, as if in search of something. By the time the boat slows at the entrance to the canal, they have stopped moving. As have the mother's gills.

~

Two decades later, I am holding my partner's hand in room seven of the Daphne ward at the Rosie Hospital, England. We have chosen the least invasive of the options available to us, a dose of misoprostol, chemical key to a medically assisted miscarriage. We are shown to a bed by a window that looks down onto a loading bay, a cold industrial alley the sun cannot reach; soon a truck will arrive, and the driver will load up the tubs of hospital refuse, and whatever else does not need to be incinerated.

Three other women lie behind curtains in the remaining corners of the room. Over the course of the day, all will take turns performing the harrowing march up and down the corridor, colluding with gravity. One of the women is violently ill for hours; her partner turns up the volume on a video game he has paid to play on the articulated wall-arm-mounted TV.

For those few minutes, the ward sounds like a casino. Later, the woman opposite begins talking in a louder voice as her neighbour begins her part, the violent nausea a side effect. This raising of voices above a whisper, to natural volume, becomes something we all do, to put each other at ease, to unburden each other of silence. Like military tacticians we are laying down a kind of covering fire, four couples hitherto unknown to each other, bound in solidarity.

My mind catches briefly on the shovelnose. And of course on my mum, who had been in a similar room, and in other kinds too, as a mother of one who didn't make it, and six that did. And if there's anything I know right now, it is this: that of all the things I wish I had been able to share with her, to talk with her about—the ego stuff, the moments of professional success, the publication of my first book, or the scholarship to Cambridge that I hope would've alleviated her well-disguised disappointment at my quitting law—this rates number one. To so many of my friends who knew her, she was a confidante, more like a cool younger aunt or even an older sister, who would know just the right thing to say. But I could only fumblingly parse her inaudible voice, what she *would* say, by periodically reassuring: *It's okay. It's okay.*

In hindsight there should've been no doubting, two nights ago. All week I had been suggesting nausea gravidarum; but by now she had guessed: 'I'm losing it, I know it.' 'Let's not write it off yet; give it a chance,' I'd said pathetically. Then the night before last, I saw it: her face in the lamplight, the strained, waxy pallor, the hint of jaundice, the soft but unmistakable whisper of mortality upon her taut skin. I had seen this before, by the light of a jaundiced moon. I should've known. I did know. And she had been right all along: the Cassandra Complex, me again. And yet, to be fair, I don't think either of us conceded until the penultimate ultrasound in the consultant's office, the once flickering heartbeat replaced by an inexplicable snowstorm.

The last to leave, we thank the nurses warmly for their kindness; hereafter, we will hold up the Rosie as a beacon of light. As we are let out, I want somehow to explain that my mum would've wholeheartedly approved, which in my book is the best compliment any maternity ward could receive. But it is late. So I hold the nurse's gaze a second longer at the door, hoping to convey something of the ineffable depths of my gratitude in silence.

∾

Valentine's Day, 1985. I am six. After tennis practice we stop in at the chemist by the school. I have a flash of inspiration and ask for two dollars, something I never do. From a display cabinet I choose one of the trinket rings with a plastic gem. My heart races as I do up my seatbelt, turn, and present the ring to my mother.

∾

En route from Siberia to its feeding grounds in New Zealand, the migrating Great Knot likes to pause at a large freshwater lagoon on the south-western shore of the island, known as Buckley's Hole. Several hundred metres inland east from Buckley's, in a clearing amid the cypress pines, there lived a hermit. He had washed up one day in 1953, in his early sixties, like a piece of flotsam after a lifetime adrift, and was content to eke out an existence in a jerry-built thatched hut until his death twenty years later in 1974 (a decade or so before we arrived). Grandpop recalled selling him fish, and said there had been rumours of 'old Ian' causing a ruckus one night during a storm, howling into the wind. Some tried to have him evicted, others excused his eccentricities on account of the fact that he was, it was said, a famous artist. Visitors came from as far away as Melbourne, writers, journalists, critics, to spend a night on the dirt floor. For it was in this studio hut—long since demolished and replaced by a commemorative plaque—that the hermit, Ian Fairweather, produced paintings 'whose emotional range and sheer breathtaking beauty', according to Robert Hughes, were 'surpassed by no other Australian picture'.

The youngest of nine, Fairweather had been left in the care of aunts in Scotland as a six-month-old, when his Surgeon General father was recalled to India in 1891. He did not see his parents or siblings again for nine years. He was a prisoner in World War I, then an art student at The Hague and in London, before becoming truly itinerant. In 1945, the year after his mother died, he bought a condemned lifeboat in Brisbane, and drifted across the bay from Sandgate and into the passage. He would return to the island eight years later, but not before first moving to Darwin, where he famously built a raft out of aircraft fuel tanks he found in a dump and, with a sail made from an old parachute canopy, set off across the Timor Sea with meagre supplies and a compass, ostensibly to visit an old friend in Indonesia. After enduring a tropical monsoon and near-certain death, he miraculously washed up on the remote island of Roti, on the edge of the Timor Sea, sixteen days later—more than a week after his obituary had

been published in Britain and Australia. The following year
he returned to Bribie Island and the passage, and built his hut
in Bongaree, not far from the favourite watering hole of the
migrating Great Knot from Siberia.

His method was to build up layer upon layer of paint—
'layers of attempt, layers of memory', Murray Bail called them.
Under a microscope, the curators of the National Gallery have
counted more than seventy in a single work. Broad strokes
overlap and all but erase moments of fine, inchoate calligraphy,
leaving tips and stems sticking out from the past, two, three,
maybe twenty versions ago of the same painting. He worked
with what lay to hand, mostly unstable surfaces, thin cardboard,
masonite, newspaper, real estate signs, which frustrated
curators. Galleries sent him canvases; he used them to repair
his hut. His style of the first decade on the island draws heavily
on Chinese calligraphy and cubism, with a hint of Matisse and
Aboriginal bark painting. He mixed mosquito-coil ash into
house paint. His subjects range from the mangroves and the
Glasshouse Mountains to scenes from his travels, but as Drusilla
Modjeska has observed, his 'single most common motif' is that
of the mother and child: 'Children with their lips glued to the
lips of the mother; babies held by the breast, sated by the breast;
babies threatened by the breast, undone by the breast.'

In *Anak Bayan* (1957), Fairweather's mother and child
motif reaches its apotheosis. A grand three-panelled work, this
depiction of a communal celebration of birth was suggested
to the artist by his time in Manila (the title means 'son of the
country' in Tagalog). In it a thin vascular calligraphy outlines
a procession of more than a dozen figures, mothers and their

children, all a mixture of dove-grey and seagull-white. Heavy strokes of umber provide shade, wisps of ochre hint at afternoon light, and there is a grounding of Prussian blue. The figures are arranged much as the Apostles are in the *Last Supper*. Two mothers in the central panel face the viewer, each with a child on her lap, like the Madonna and child; they are surrounded by other permutations of maternal intimacy: the child rocking back on the knee, the child with hands in the air, the child walking by the mother's hip. While the motif was evident in his work from the thirties, it was only once the artist had settled on the island, with the raft episode behind him, that it returned to consume him. More often than not, as in *Anak Bayan*, the child's fingers are oddly shaped, like paws or claws, either clinging, digging into his mother's flesh—or longing to.

~

Two types of scrambling vine clamber along the dunes on the surf side of the island. There is the beach morning glory, whose mauve flowers bear dark pink throats; and the more vigorous climbing guinea flower, or snake vine, which blossoms with five large petals of golden yellow, and whose new leaves look as though they were covered in cotton wool. The seeds of the former come in papery capsules, like individually wrapped gobstoppers, while the red fleshy seeds of the latter are dehiscent, their pods bursting open at the moment of maturity. When a king tide threatens to delete the island overnight, gouging the dunes with dozer-sized scoops, the metres-long runners remain dangling from the overhang, as if waiting to catch new earth.

Playing bedlam in the dunes as a kid, you often trip over them, an ankle snared. On a quieter day you might pick one to trace to its source, charting it through the tangle of hundreds of its fellows. The trick is to pull it up so that each shallow anchor root stapling the runner to the sand pops off in succession; when the vine is taut, you can see more clearly where it is bound. If the dune is steep, it is easy to get distracted by becoming a SWAT soldier: the rugged vines making perfect grappling ropes with which to scale the walls of an enemy sand compound. Then there are the times you think you've traced one of the runners through a maze of spinifex to its source, only to see that it continues again, impossibly this time, through a room-sized bloom of beach primrose. So you run down to join the games in the sea instead, content to leave the mystery of the tough vine's source unresolved.

A bright summer's day, in what must be early 1979. The four of us, at the base of the Opera House steps, not far from where *Anak Bayan* is kept in the Art Gallery of New South Wales. On the right, Nan in a nurse-blue dress has turned her back; Pop in a pale grey collared shirt, sleeves rolled up, tucked smartly into pressed mauve flares (I don't remember him like this!), a trim figure in profile, also turning away. Off-centre, to the left, I am in a pram; my months-old arms reach towards her as she looks at the camera, in a high-waisted ivory pleated skirt, slightly transparent in the sun, and white short-sleeved blouse. Her left hand rests on the hood of the pram, her right by her side, cigarette held casually. Brilliant, open-toed crimson heels, ankle-strapped, make her as tall as her father; matching red lipstick graces her mouth, her jaw set ever so slightly with . . . is it defiance? I have seen this look more recently, in my younger sister's face.

The photo is one of more than fifty to arrive in the post out of the blue six weeks ago from my biological father who, until last year, I hadn't spoken to since I was four, and could not remember beyond a shadow. One night on a whim eighteen months ago my partner had googled his name, and found a match with the first initial and surname. The match played in a regular poker tournament in Chatswood, one suburb from where my birth certificate says I was born. (Mum had led us to believe that he would likely have moved back to Jakarta; the poker website seemed to suggest that he had not moved at all.)

Several months after this discovery of a possible candidate for the biological father I never imagined I would see again, I happened to be in Sydney on a night the tournament was due to take place. Taking an old school mate along with me for support, I thought we'd arrive early to set up somewhere with a good view and see if we could pick him out. A queue was already forming at the registration desk.

'I'm not living in Australia at the moment,' I explained. 'I'm signing in because I'm hoping to meet an old friend who I haven't seen for years, and who I know plays poker here. The thing is, we haven't seen each other for so long that we might not even recognise each other.' I could have been a debt collector, or worse.

'Sure, what's his name?' came the reply.

I gave the name. The woman repeated it.

'Yes', she said slowly, before glancing beyond me, to the queue. 'Oh! You mean the guy standing behind you?' she said, pointing.

As I turned, he was already emerging from the middle of the small mass of bodies, like a Pollock blue pole from the surrounding noise. He looked at me, then at the staff, then said in accented English, 'Someone say my name?'

My plan of arriving early and being in control of the situation suddenly evaporated.

'Yes. I did. Ah, I'm hoping to ask you a question,' I said, before adding, 'but you should sign in first.'

I wandered over to my school mate, who was beaming. 'He looks like you,' he said.

I knew it too, but I had to make sure. Moments later I was stepping forward to meet him as he approached from the registration desk. For some reason I began by assuring him that we didn't know each other, before asking whether he remembered having known a woman with my mother's name. He looked down for a moment, then up again, this time locking my gaze.

'Yes.'

I asked him if he was sure. He confirmed that he was. Then I told him my first name.

'So you're. You're . . .!' he said.

'Yes.'

'You're my *son*!'

'Yes.'

'You found me! H-h-how you find me? I always wonder if you find me!'

'The poker tournament.'

'You play poker!' he marvelled, before entreating my mate and me to have a drink with him. We found a table, and my mate went to get some beers.

'I can't believe it. All this time.'

'I know!'

'And how *is* Debbie?'

I feel that in some sense we are even, he and I. I can never know my mum's life in that photo, though I am in it; and he will never know how she filled her children with awe one day by paddling to the mainland and back on a surf ski, as if it were a cinch, setting out from a small patch of sand to which I would also later return—hoping to forget, so that I might remember.

A TALE OF TWO FATHERS

KATHRYN HEYMAN

WHEN YOU LIVE ACROSS THE OCEAN, you learn to fear the ringing of the telephone after midnight, the email marked URGENT, the harsh awakening with the dry-mouth panic. Even in half-sleep you know that they only call at two am when something has gone wrong; when there is nothing to be done. My suitcase is packed, waiting on the landing. I have a flight to Sydney booked, ready to leave in two days' time. I know he's going. Three months, that's what they told me.

My sister echoes down the line from Sydney, her voice cold and strange: 'He's going.'

'I know. Three months. He's got three months.' I know why she's called, why she's bothered rousing me from sleep, but if I keep talking, speaking over her, explaining my flight details—here I am now, pulling the printed itinerary from the suitcase, shouting it down the phone—'No, *listen*! Jesus, why do you never listen to me? I'm flying from Glasgow in two days, I'll stay overnight in London, then my flight leaves at . . .' I squint at the paper in the dull light from the hallway lamp.

She's crying. 'He's worse. You have to talk to him.'

'He can't go. He has to wait. Tell him he has to wait.'

She hands the phone to the nurse. I can still hear her crying.

I say, 'Tell him that he can fucking well wait. Tell him that for once in his life he can think about me instead of himself. Jesus.'

There is silence on the other end.

Silence has always been part of my communication with my father. He has never been good at talking. Or embracing. Or making eye contact. In 1996 Asperger's syndrome is still unmentioned outside academic papers. All we know is that our father has spent his life avoiding us. When my mother left him—after the bruises got too large to cover up—I was six years old. In spite of the bruises, family lore has it that I spent months pining for him so much that I was physically ill, holding my belly, saying, 'I'm homesick for Daddy.' It was a homesickness for a father, a pining over a permanent absence which I thought would never be healed. But I was wrong.

This is the story of two fathers, not one.

Sheffield, in the north of England, is a city that feels like a market town, folded into the green valleys and brown hills of the Peak District National Park. The city is famous for steel and for Jarvis Cocker. In our house it's famous for being the site of the beginning of our love story. Sheffield in 1993 is loud and vibrant, full of promise. On the day I move into my student share house in the south of the city, I meet Richard in the hallway. Three months later he brings John, his father, to a pub poetry reading where I read poems and sing, accompanying myself very badly on a battered guitar. Later, the three of us sit up in the kitchen late into the night, drinking weak tea and talking about books and education. *Talking. About books.* I last saw my own father in 1990, when I'd had my first play produced. Puffed with pride, I flew to Sydney, drove to Tamworth and ate dinner with him. I said, 'I've had a play produced. By a mainhouse theatre company. I'm writing another one.'

My father said, 'Oh? I've got to go over tomorrow to have a look at the horses. You can come with me. We'll take the back roads.'

When John leaves Sheffield the next morning, setting off for a three-hour drive back to Chester, he holds his son close in a hug that lasts minutes, not seconds. He keeps his hands on Richard's shoulders, steps back and says, 'I love you. You are an extraordinary young man. I wish your mother was still alive to see you.' I sneak a sideways glance at Richard, checking to see if he's embarrassed by this extravagant show of affection. A father hugging a son? Saying 'I love you' out loud? A sharpness twists inside me, a mixture of fear and envy. Beside me, Richard beams at his father, waving him off, basking in the certainty of being loved and being considered exceptional.

He is exceptional in fact—not least because his easy, loving relationship with his father gives him an unusual solidity of character—and eighteen months later, I marry him. My father doesn't send a card.

I was in Sheffield when my father was diagnosed with lung cancer. A horse-breaking policeman, he'd smoked for most of his life and harboured the kind of deep rage that now, years later, I suspect comes from being unable to deeply connect with another human being. As a child, before my mother found the courage from God-knows-where to leave him, I remember the women on the street who smiled slowly at my father, rested their hands on his arm, pushed their chests towards him. Two police officers came to my kindy class to talk about the Good Work of the Force. Desperately keen, I thrust my hand in the air, shouted, 'My dad is a policeman. He's the boss of Boolaroo.' The young lady officer—in my memory she is brunette, snub-nosed and lightly freckled, but I am only truly certain of the nose—smiled down at me. 'What's his name?' When I shouted out my father's name, the officer blushed; her male companion snorted. Before she left, the policewoman said, 'Give your dad a kiss for me,' and as my beautiful soft-faced kindy teacher bustled the officers out the door, I felt the terrible burn of shame on my own face.

I adored my father then; longed for his face to be turned to me, only me. I hated that lady officer. She had a stupid nose and her gun wasn't even real.

～

In Sheffield, after his diagnosis, I begin writing a novel about a horse-breaking policeman in Boolaroo, New South Wales, and his inability to feel anything except rage. My father haunts my dreams. I wake at night, sweating, and cross out the pages. In the morning, I salvage the pages and tell myself that he will never read them, no one will ever read them. Anyway, it's fiction. This story has two sisters, a fierce angry one and a simple 'special' one who wears calipers and is cross-eyed and adores everyone. I am one of five, not two. And although I was called Clarence the Cross-eyed Lion and although I wore calipers—a possible side effect of being housed in a womb which was housed in a belly which sometimes got in the way of a wall or a fist—I did not go to Special School. And although we had a prison in the backyard where the local drunks were locked up, my childhood backyard prison did not house Jack, a drunken hymn-singer and giver of dead flowers. So there's really no question. It's fiction.

Richard's father spends weekends with us, takes us to lunch, to National Trust properties. 'How amazing,' he says to me, 'how amazing that you are writing a novel. Wonderful. Creativity is so courageous.'

When I graduate he buys me a silver ink pen, engraved with my name, and an antique pen stand. In the card, he writes: *Mightier than the sword!*

Richard and I marry in Chester, an Easter wedding. My father has had lung cancer for eighteen months. I write aerogramme letters to him each week and every few months I get a paragraph or two back from my stepmother: *Your father is continuing to be well. He has two new mares. He sends his best regds.*

My father-in-law makes the speech at our wedding, praising both of us and our love story. He says, 'I am so glad to have this new daughter.' In my speech, I do not say, 'I am so glad to have this new father.' But I am.

John's wedding gift to us is a honeymoon in Australia; a chance for Richard to see my homeland, to view my childhood without the prism of my novel-in-progress. And to meet my father.

I call him when we arrive in Australia. He says, 'I'm going to drive up to Lemon Tree Passage to see Aunty Sissy. You can come with me.'

I say, 'No. I don't want to go to Lemon Tree Passage. I don't even know Aunty Sissy. Why can't you just come and have lunch with me? I want you to meet Richard.'

Silence for a moment, then, 'Where do you want to go for lunch? Chinese?'

We don't go to the Toronto Main Road Chinese (or 'Chinky' as my father would have it). I have spent years trying to meet him on his own terms, years writing to him with no reply, years travelling to the stupid places that he chooses to live, years putting up with the bitter wife and her pet galah, and this time, just for once, we can bloody well eat what I want to eat and I want focaccia.

My father has never heard of focaccia. How ludicrous I am with my fancy London food. I tell him that we have lived in Glasgow, not London, since we married. London, Glasgow, same thing, he says. All fancy schmancy.

The cafe is overcrowded and the street noise means that we have to lean close to hear. I show my father a wedding photo.

He says it's nice. He doesn't make eye contact with Richard. Our knees touch and I ask Dad how the treatment is going. Fine, he says. Can't get rid of me that easily. When the menu comes he scans it, bewildered. I have never seen him small, my father, never lost like this. Or never noticed, perhaps that's it. He was always so large in my memory and in my imagination.

He doesn't ask me any questions, not one. Curiosity about my life, about anything, is beyond him. I tell myself it's okay, that I don't need him to see me, to notice me.

Back in Glasgow, the winter sets in. My father-in-law spends Christmas with us and we walk in the woods near Loch Lomond, stunned by a loamy golden light. He asks about Australia, about my father. I say he's not a great man, that there's not really much else to say. My father-in-law says, 'But he produced a great daughter.'

John's gift is encouragement. Where my own father cannot notice other people's achievements, John is unable to see their failures. A primary school head teacher, he glories in noticing the fine moments when people do well. On a cool spring day we visit a cathedral in the south, lush with the dank smell of stone and age. Absorbed in reading the plaque above a soldier's tomb, I feel Richard sidle alongside me—sense the warmth of him rather than see him—and without turning my head I slip my arm through his companionably. Laughter echoes against the stone, and the stranger whose arm I have slipped mine through tries to back away. John smiles at the stranger and says, 'You have just been accosted by Kathryn Heyman. Upcoming author.

She's a great talent. You should remember her name, you'll be dining out on it in years to come.' I pretend mortification, but I am delighted of course; delighted in the way a child is delighted. This is new to me, having an elder notice me, praise me, spur me on to meet my potential. In newsagents, supermarkets, cafes, John chats to strangers, boasting of my spurious achievements, or his son's, his daughter's, his brother's. Where my own father likes to pull people down with that slightly bitter deprecation that in a certain sort of Australian man passes for humour— *What? You on a horse? You'll have to spend a month on bread and water first, hey Fatty?*—John loves to build them up. Sometimes I berate him for it, this foolish, blind positivity—and it does cause real injury, too, years later, his inability to see people's flaws, his unwillingness to read their darker motives. But in these years I become like Richard, basking in his father's unconditional regard, and the wound I have carried all these years, the painful aching homesickness, begins to close over with barely a scar.

The novel I began writing in Sheffield has taken on a furious life and I spend each night hunched over the keyboard, tapping out the dim ghosts of my childhood. When the Scottish Arts Council gives me a fellowship, a card arrives in the letterbox with a picture of a ship in full sail. It's from my father-in-law, a 'well done' card. The kind of thing a father would do, the kind of thing you hope a father would do. Inside, written in his scratchy crooked writing, eked out with the half-broken calligraphy pen he insists on using: *You are on course! I am so very proud of you.* When Richard is awarded his doctorate, John's applause fills the theatre. Unaffected, uncomplicated pride and pleasure in the achievements of others. It's not so strange, I suppose. People express such sentiments all the time. But not in the house of my childhood, the house that I am calling back to life in my novel. My father's fury is in there, the prison in the backyard is there, the horses being wooed and charmed and hurt until they are broken—they are in there. But watching my father throw my six-year-old brother across the room as the little boy tries to protect my mother, that is not there. It's my most vivid childhood memory, my brave dark-skinned brother running across the linoleum floor, clinging to my mother's legs and shouting, 'Stop it! Just stop it!' and then his body strangely floppy, like a rag doll (my older sister had one called Renata, red-cheeked and pink-lipped, and I wanted Renata for myself), and there he is, flipping through the air, again and again and again in my memory and sometimes in my dreams. I don't remember him landing. I don't remember him crying. I remember he didn't try to stop my father after that.

Here are my husband's memories of his father: taking a small wooden boat to a lake in Norwich, waiting for hours for the perfect wind until it finally set sail; playing Monopoly in the midst of a storm, sucking sweets that are still, now, stuck to the Monopoly board; building dams in Welsh rivers; words, lots of words—*good boy*, *well done*, *you're doing well*, *who's my best boy?*—those words of course, but others too, words about books, stories, history, jokes, nonsense, nothings, everythings. The words that allow a child to blossom.

The furious novel is almost finished. I've signed with my dream agent and I am breathless with anticipation and terror.

What will my father say? What will any of them say? I lie awake staring at the ceiling, knowing I can never finish it, knowing I will be punished if I do. My new agent takes me to a raucous lunch in Edinburgh and the next day my sister calls from London. She's had a call from another sister, who was called by the galah-owning stepmother. My sister says, 'It's progressed to secondaries. It's in his kidneys. They're saying three months. I'm flying out tomorrow.'

Perhaps she says, 'three months, tops'. Or, 'up to three months'. In the days and months and years to follow I play it over again in my mind, that call, my response. But each time, I'm sure that's what I hear: three months, they're saying three months.

Between us, Richard and I have a total of six hundred pounds in the bank, so I book the soonest, cheapest flight possible, the only one I can afford, with a company running charter holidays to Australia. The flight leaves in eight days.

For six days I am suspended. What do you do when you are waiting for a flight to take you to say goodbye to the father who never was a father, the father you love, the father you hate? My novel is fat and accusatory on my desk. I cover it with a towel, like a dead person. And then I wait.

In the winter just gone, Glasgow had been snowed in. The whole city, covered with snow so thick that cars were abandoned in the middle of the street. Everything was muffled, suspended. Regular services cancelled. Theatres and libraries closed, trains not running. Everyone huddled in under a blanket of quiet and waiting. This, now, this waiting, it's like being snowed in.

Muffled and suspended. I don't know what to do. My cases are packed, my tickets issued. Everything seems foolish, pointless. I sit in my study playing endless games of Tetris, then move downstairs to watch videos of *The X-Files*. Then Tetris again. I can almost hear my own breathing.

And then, the call, the two am stumble to the landing, my sister sobbing in the hospital ward, the silence.

Finally, the nurse says, 'He's here. The phone is beside his bed. I'll put him on.'

And so I speak to him, my father, for the last time, saying goodbye across the world. He rouses himself to pull out more words than he's ever given me in a final rallying, a brief flutter of being a father. I say it again, barely able to speak, hiccuping down the phone, I say, 'Please, Dad, please wait. I'm on my way, I really am.'

He says, 'I have to go, Bloss.'

Blossom. It was his name for me when I was a pigtailed child in Boolaroo, New South Wales, Australia. I'd forgotten that.

He hands the phone back to the nurse, or perhaps he drops it on the hospital bed and she picks it up. I am not there and I have to fill these gaps in myself from what I know, from what happens on my end of the phone. The nurse says, 'He's tired.'

'He's saying goodbye. He's going.' My words string together, wet and mucousy.

'No, no. He's tired. He meant he had to go, get off the phone.'

'No. He meant he had to leave life.'

And then I can't speak any more, so I hang up the phone and put my face on the stair above me and I sob into the ugly brown carpet. Fifteen minutes later, on the other side of the world, my father makes a snoring sound, swallows, and then stops breathing.

In the morning, another call, this time to my father's wife. She is weary and wary. The funeral will be held two days before my flight is due to arrive. She says she can't wait for me. Won't. I phone the airline: could they change my flight? Get me on an earlier one? Today? They're sorry, terribly sorry, but that ticket cannot be changed. Sympathetically, the woman on the end of the phone clucks, 'You really do have to be careful with cheaper tickets.'

My father-in-law buys me a new ticket back to Australia.

We get to Glasgow Airport as the transfer flight to London is boarding. The woman at the counter—brownish-blonde hair scraped back tightly—says, 'I'm sorry, hen. The flight has boarded. You'll hae to get the next flight.'

The woman beside her is English, or at least does a fair impression of a southern accent. She clocks me with my greasy hair, my wild eyes, and she says, 'Check-in has closed.'

Glasgow's airport is very small. I can see the last of the passengers walking through to the gate.

The English woman repeats, more carefully, 'Check-in has closed.'

Her companion says helpfully, 'Ye can buy another one for later.'

I heave my suitcase up onto the counter and explain that I have to catch this flight so that I can get the connecting flight to Sydney, Australia. To get to my father's funeral. My father who has just died, this morning. I say this slowly, and breathing deeply, to help the folk of Loganair understand the weight of the matter.

'Check-in has closed.' This time she flicks her scarf about her neck as an exclamation point.

I say, 'My father has just died. If you don't let me on that flight I will be laying myself down here all night where I will wail and scream and sob. I will do that loudly and you will have to arrest me to get rid of me.'

You think English people don't like scenes? Scottish people, for all their reputation of wild fights in the streets, like them even less. The mess of them, the awkwardness of all those feelings.

She lets me on the flight.

Tamworth is baking, heat bubbling up from footpaths thronged by the crowds in town for the country music festival. Out of town, the crematorium is rose-addled and oddly green. Someone plays the Last Post. His coffin is draped with a flag and his Akubra; never one to go unhatted, my father. There is much talk of what a man he was, what a great man, a giver to the community, a great horseman. There is no mention of my mother, the wife he hurt for twenty years, and there is little mention of us, his five children. I sit halfway towards the back of the crematorium with my feet pressed together and my skin burning into a deep angry red rash. Later, the five of us gather under a pale eucalypt in the wind. There is a photo somewhere; each of us clinging to the other, unsure whether to smile for the camera, the spare flat of the crematorium gardens spread behind us. It's rare for us to be together, we want to mark it, note it down. There we are, held together by loss.

When I return home to Scotland, my face and my arms are covered with red lumps. The doctor gives me cortisone but says there is no explanation for the rash. My sister tells me it's my body letting all the rage out and gives me a Louise L Hay book: *You Can Heal Your Life*. I tell her to fuck off and then I throw a mug at the wall.

So I'm not sure that the rage is gone.

The end of the novel comes easily after all that. I know what's needed now, I know what was missing all those years. Now I know how to make a moment of redemption, of possibility—in life as well as in fiction. Because I am not, in the end, merely my father's daughter.

Late spring, there is an auction for the book, redemptive ending and all. My father-in-law drives up to Glasgow, spends a week with us, celebrating my success. He comes to the Groucho Club with us, gives my agent a history of the building and tells him not to drink so much. He reads the books I give him, delights in the successes of my friends. He walks through the door of my world with loving curiosity.

When I thought about writing this piece, this story of my father's death and his final words to me, this is what I imagined: explaining how I had been given a second father. Then, I would give it to my father-in-law to read. Here, I would say. You are my father, you have been more than my father. And I am grateful.

Instead, there is another phone call. Another flight across the sea. Another night spent sobbing beneath a blanket on a plane.

This time I am in Ubud, Bali. I have spent the afternoon speaking to aspiring writers in a pamper-rich resort. Mid-afternoon, one of the writers asks me about desire in fiction. 'Can the desire be what your character *doesn't* want?'

'Nope.' It's the end of the day, I have no time for wavering, so perhaps I am snappy. 'You can't *un*want something. That would be ridiculous.'

But once more, I am wrong.

At the end of the session, I check my email. There's a message from Richard, the subject titled URGENT. *Call me immediately. Cancel whatever you are doing and call now.* I haven't been able to get my phone working in Bali, so I use the resort phone, stammering out my request to call Australia. It cuts out twice before I get to hear a complete sentence. This time, it's Richard who can barely speak.

It was sudden, for John. There was no waiting and no chance for a final goodbye. He had a quick, brutal stroke and died that night. There are no last words.

Balinese heat sways around me as I stand in the middle of a bright, rich garden, curling over, weeping down the line to Australia.

It's a strange replaying: the argument with the airline to get on a flight, the mad run to the airport, my sense of a thin grip on sanity. Running through Denpasar Airport, trailing luggage behind me, I push past a couple who shout, 'Oi! Watch it!' I keep running, attempting to shout something over my shoulder that will help them understand my rush, my panic, my distress. Only one word comes out, shrieked at the two of them as I push past more travellers. 'Dead!' I shriek. 'Dead!' Later, on the plane, I blush. My father-in-law would have been appalled at my lack of manners. He'd have stopped, had a chat, explained the history of Denpasar to them, and then ticked off the airline staff for closing the gates early. But all that's done now, and it's not fair, it's not fair.

Richard leaves for London as soon as I arrive in Sydney. In the past decade John has remarried someone with a nuclear share of bitterness and damage, and we worry that she will make the funeral difficult for our children, that we won't be welcome. So I stay home, and Richard flies through the night, red-eyed and heart-sore. At the airport, Richard says, 'The degree to which I am a good father is because of the example I had in him. All my memories of my father in childhood and into young adulthood, all of them are good, positive, loving memories. Whatever happens now, in his death, can't undo that. The choices he made in these last years can't undo that. It won't.'

I take the children to a beachside hotel up the coast and we write messages in the sand, letting the water wash them away. I notice myself framing photos to send him, drafting messages. For almost twenty years he has been an applauding audience to my life. Who will be my audience now?

When Richard returns, we spend night after night lying alongside each other talking, talking, talking until we are dry. Exhausted, hoping for some light relief, we download a movie. *The Visitor*, it turns out, is not a witty reflection on immigration, but a profound reflection on grief. At the end of the film, the central character—a held-in college professor who has lost everyone he has cared about—walks down to the subway with a djembe drum. Loosening his tie, he begins to play, his hands flapping, his tie swinging. We lie next to each other, plank-like, heavy with sadness, my head on Richard's chest. On the screen, while subway trains pull in and leave, the professor beats out a rhythm with greater and greater ferocity. Beneath my head, Richard's heart is pounding—*dum dada dum, dum dada dum*—faster, fiercer. The beat plays into my sleep. *I unwant this. I unwant this.*

At the end of life, there is only what you are capable of giving. At the end of his life, my father—unseeing, incapable, incurious—lay on a hospital bed ten thousand miles from me. He asked the nurse for some water and then he said, 'Bloss, I'm sorry. I wasn't the best. I know I wasn't.' He took some more water, and on my dark stairwell in Glasgow, I cried some more. Then he said, 'You've done so well. And I know everything you've done, you've done it yourself. You've made yourself. And you should be proud.'

Then he said, 'I have to go now.'

That was it. That was my moment of perfect redemption; the words that spilled so easily from John could only be wrenched from my father by death. It doesn't undo his years of failure, any more than failures at the end undo a life of praise and gratitude. But I am grateful for those words, I am grateful he had a moment of grace and that he could pass it on to me. He was wrong, though. I did not make myself, did not become myself alone.

I am, at the very least, the product of two fathers.

AFTERLIFE

DAVID MARR

THEIR DEATHS WERE AWFUL. Dad was a fair-skinned surfer. Mum was a smoker. A young GP gave my father his death sentence: the melanomas cut out years before were back and nothing could be done. As I drove him home he said perfectly seriously: 'This is going to kill your mother.' But she would carry on, a game old woman with no flesh on her bones, determined to live as she had for as long as she could. Smoking was one of the loves of her life. 'When we were courting, your father handed me a Turf and said "You might like one of these," and I did.' She didn't blame him at all. Her brand was Du Maurier but she later switched to Benson & Hedges. British was best with her: British clothes, British accents, British books, British cigarettes. We fetched them for her. We lit them and took a puff when she was driving. We emptied the ashtrays. Dad gave up but she ploughed on. By my rough calculation she had smoked three hundred and fifty thousand by the time a bad heart forced her to go cold turkey at the age of sixty-nine. Twelve years later she couldn't shake off a dry cough.

Because there was no hope for either of them, we wanted it over quickly. We didn't want them dead but we wanted them to die. Yet as cancer ate away, they seemed indestructible. 'I'm not enjoying this,' my father remarked when he emerged from a morphine stupor one afternoon. Days later I heard him say: 'Give up, heart. Give up.' His dying was like a long sleepless night. The hours passed very slowly. He often asked the time and it was never late enough. He was tormented by hallucinations. 'Son, tell me, are rats running around the mirror?' He kept his eye on two clocks: the little electric one by his bed and the old clock ticking all our lives in the hall. He rang me once or twice to come to the house and fiddle with the pendulum to keep the two in synch. Accuracy was his lifelong passion. He was an engineer, a mathematician. 'All that's left,' he said quietly one afternoon, 'is to work towards zero.'

I had no unfinished business with him. All the great disputes we had when I was young had been resolved. I risked everything in my twenties telling him who I was. That was absolutely fine. My career was a mystery to him but he accepted that too. He faced facts and taught us to do the same. I loved him profoundly. We all did. I have an older brother, Andrew, and two younger sisters, Annabel in the city and Jane, a doctor in the bush. Not until we came within sight of the finishing line did I see how difficult Jane's position became. We were all taking our cues from her: the family, the nurses and his GP. She was not his doctor but she was in charge. I did what I do, took notes.

Wednesday

He was back at work, worried about an order for Pyrmont. Transverse sections. The bishop came in the afternoon. We had tea and discussed texts. Mum wanted the funeral to be right. No false sentiment, no intrusion into the family's privacy, some brake on religiosity. Her old friend the bishop was her guarantee. She'd baked coconut biscuits and put out the silver. He asked if he could go in to Dad and pray. Mum agreed. I watched him go into the bedroom and Dad said, 'Don,' and shook his hand. I went into the kitchen but my niece appeared a few moments later and said we were all wanted in the bedroom. We stood around Dad's bed with the bishop bowing over him. It was a good prayer. We were all in tears. Dad said a breathy amen and there was a fusillade of weeping in the room. The bishop left.

A guy called Alex arrived with an oxygen machine and gave complicated instructions. But as the thing was being set up in the study—with a long green tube to the bed delivering air into Dad's nose via two prongs—Jane was already on the phone first to the doctor, then the hospital and then the ambulance. She'd decided he had gone too far downhill to be at home that night. We were all relieved, even Dad, that the decision had been made. Jane told him it might only be for a night, just to get him stabilised. Mum packed his overnight bag: razor, brush, change of pyjamas etc. His boxes and bottles of pills were put in a plastic bag. The ambulance arrived about six. Two quiet, direct guys wearing rubber gloves wheeled their trolley into the bedroom. We shifted furniture. They slid him onto the trolley and out to the ambulance. He lay very high under the neon light in the back. Jane rode with him. She said one of the men apologised to Dad for having to take his blood pressure. Dad said, very clearly, he was to do it and not to worry. I brought Mum in the car. We arrived a few minutes after the ambulance and were sent to a television room while they got Dad ready. We made tea, ate dry biscuits and watched the seven o'clock ABC news. Then they called us.

Dad was in a five-bed ward, calm, with oxygen up his nose. He was polite to the last. A nurse asked if he would like sandwiches for tea. Yes. And a cup of tea? Yes. We must have looked amazed. She asked us, 'Would he like coffee instead?' We laughed and explained he hadn't eaten solids for a week or so, nor had tea for weeks. She left and returned with a little vanilla milkshake with Sustagen. Dad drank some. Mum said, 'It's Sustagen.' Dad said bluntly, 'It's not Sustagen.' Across the ward an old man with a plaintive English accent begged to be let out of bed. I started to give him a hand before I realised he couldn't move. He was tied to his bed with a catheter on his dick. I swung his legs back in. He moaned and protested through the night. The nurses dealt with him patiently, like a child. The only other sound in the ward during the night was a soft but urgent Italian voice somewhere calling, 'Ex-cuss-a-me, ex-cuss-a-me.'

Dad was out of it. There was no conversation. After a little time we left to have dinner. 'See you in the morning,' Drew said and he replied, 'Right, see you in the morning.' Back at the house, Jane called me out of the dining room and asked if I would go back and sit with him. She was worried. Being distressed is a sign of life but Dad was now so calm. 'I think he might die tonight.'

When I got back about ten-fifteen he was breathing loudly.

I sat in the dark holding his hand. He had a strong grip on mine. A couple of times he pulled the oxygen line out to rub his nose with his knuckles—he's always scratched his nose that way—and I put the prongs back in, telling him it was me. He was quite agitated. I called a nurse. They put a 'butterfly' into the skin of his chest to inject him. As she opened his pyjamas she said, 'No hair.' I thought she was giving him a breakthrough dose of morphine but it was a sedative. She checked with her torch the dilation of his pupils. He quietened down.

I asked for a torch to read by. They gave me one but a little later brought a reading light. I settled down with a new novel, *The Glass Palace* by Amitav Ghosh. I was only half reading. My eyes slid all over the pages. I never finished it and never want to. I held Dad's hand through the bars of the bed. His breathing was company. I was scared of him dying on my watch. Doubted he would. Wished he would. Afraid he might. My fear was cold and gentle.

Thursday
About one-thirty am the nurse looked in through the curtains and said, 'Oh, I forgot. A couple of hours ago your sister rang to say to call her if you need to be relieved.' Which sister? She couldn't remember the name. Did she sound city or country? She couldn't say. 'She sounded normal.' I thought, there is going to be trouble here if I don't ring but I can't wake everyone to find out who it was.

The oxygen was annoying him and he very precisely removed the tubes from his face. The nurse put a peg of some kind on his finger and decided the level of oxygen was okay, so the tank was turned off. Dad started counting: 'Thirty-eight, thirty-nine, forty, forty-one.' Sometimes only a couple of numbers; sometimes they were out of order. These may have been the war years. He grew agitated again and they sedated him again.

Somewhere between two and three he started to gurgle, breathing heavily. He was also twitching. I called the nurse. She thought the twitching was dreams but said they could give him something to dry out the gurgling, though it might dry out his mouth too much at the same time. After hesitating a little while they gave him a shot, again through the butterfly. Her torch wasn't working well so I held the reading light for her to check his pupils. They offered me a bed, reassured me he was okay and I said, still believing it, 'He's got a few days left in him.' I was crying in bursts. At some point I said to him, 'You can go. You can go.'

About four-thirty he was agitated again and this time they rang the hospital doctor and the nurse gave a third, stronger, dose of sedatives through the butterfly. Again, he calmed down quickly. His hands were crossed over his chest. The gurgling was very loud. Sometime after five there was a sudden change in the rhythm of his breathing. He wasn't digging down deep with each breath. I called the nurse. She checked his pulse. She knew what was on my mind: I could ring people, she said, but his pulse was strong. 'It's too early.'

I decided I would ring the house either at six or when I finished the book, whichever was sooner. I was telling the time all night by Dad's watch. But at six I was afraid to move. There was a public phone in the hall—I'd used it the night before—

but I hadn't yet taken in the obvious fact that there was also a little phone on his bedside table. He stopped breathing. I pressed the buzzer. Luckily the nurses thought this was the troublesome English guy and ignored the call. So I was alone for this. Dad was lying straight in his bed with his hands crossed over his chest. I had my hands on his. Often in the last week he had not breathed for a stretch. This was a very long stretch. His face was absolutely still with his mouth hanging open. Then there was a little breath and a long silence. By his watch it was six-ten.

I found the phone. Rang Jane and said come. Dad gave a soft, long fart. That was it. I rang Annabel and couldn't say he was dead, just come to the hospital. Couldn't remember Drew's number and had to ring directory assistance. Didn't have a pen. A nurse appeared. She asked if I was all right. I was and said so. She asked if she should close Dad's mouth with a towel rolled under his chin. I said no. She left. I found his brush in the drawer beside the bed and brushed his hair. I kissed him on the forehead when it was done. He looked milky pale. I don't think I cried. Outside there was a burst of noise from birds—lorikeets, I think—and then it was quiet again. The nurse brought me a mug of tea.

I sat with him. At six-thirty Mum's and Jane's feet appeared under the curtain. Mum sat on the far side of the bed. I said, 'He just stopped breathing.' Mum asked, 'Is he breathing now?' Jane said, 'No, Mum.' I made tea for them. I went out and walked up and down the road for a bit. It was a beautiful early autumn morning. There was a woman rushing down the hill to the station. I wanted to yell: It doesn't matter!

Drew arrived and went inside to say his goodbyes and do what had to be done. We sat in the sun waiting for Annabel. An hour passed. We wanted to be gone. The nurses knocked off from their shift. They were surprised how quickly he had gone. His pulse had been strong. The twitching had not been dreams, it seems, but a sign he was dying. Annabel arrived. Mum had packed Dad's things. I went to pick up a pair of green viyella pyjamas on the bedside table. Mum said, 'Leave those. They always wonder what to dress people in.' He should have had his overalls.

I went back to the television/tearoom for a few moments and came back to find him alone. Mum had left. A nurse with rubber gloves was about to start work on the body. She shook my hand then evaporated. I kissed Dad again on the forehead and said goodbye. Mum was in the vestibule. I hugged her and she flinched. She looked terrible but was holding herself upright. A nurse appeared and slipped Dad's watch into her hand. She had trouble finding somewhere for it in her handbag. It disappeared. We left.

The days that followed had their horrors. We righted ourselves. My brother, a born oldest son, did everything well. The bishop held to his side of the unspoken bargain: my father was buried, not as a Christian but a decent man. Men from the works came to the wake to talk affectionately about the old days and Mr George. We threw his ashes off the rocks where he used to fish at Whale Beach and as we climbed back up the cliff a pod of dolphins swam by paying their respects.

My mother's pretence that little had changed served us all well. But her life was broken. My parents had adored each other. Even in old age they still thought themselves lucky to have met. He protected her. 'Don't upset your mother,' was one of his tougher commands. She was the centre of attention but he had the authority. At the age of seventy-eight she was batting on without much of the reason for her life. Something shifted in her. This deeply conventional woman—indeed, an authority on doing all things right—seemed not to care so much any more about the verdict of the golf club. It was a relief to her. She was funny and unexpected. 'What you want to know,' she announced combatively one afternoon, 'is whether I went to the altar a virgin.' We did. She had. Her days were long. She kept saying as she had all our lives: 'We must keep an eye on the time.' But there was less and less reason. She had the housework done by nine am and cooked us the same ghost meals we'd laughed about for years: great recipes reduced ingredient by 'unnecessary' ingredient to shadows of themselves. She kept a stern watch on the upbringing of her grandchildren.

No one mentioned the little cough. A bad shoulder drove her from the court. After playing tennis for something like seventy-five years, she wasn't going to suffer the indignity of serving underarm. The pain grew worse. X-rays showed a mass in her left lung. She knew what it was. 'I could operate,' said the young man who had given my father his death sentence only a couple of years before. 'I don't think so,' she replied. He offered chemotherapy. 'No. We won't do anything about this.' She knew she was going the same hard way my father had gone. She stuck to all the old routines. Suddenly breathless one afternoon, she was taken to hospital and never came out. She shrank. When she could no longer swallow she was sent to see a surgeon. The driver lost his way navigating the suburbs where she had lived all her life. This was my mother's territory. At death's door, her last triumph was to show the driver the back way from Wahroonga to Hornsby.

Annabel kept smoking. 'This,' she told me in the hospital garden one morning, 'is no time to give up cigarettes.' Later she did. One day she brought good news that had to be kept absolutely secret for a week. My mother, a gossip absurdly sure of her discretion, made all the right promises but the first nurse into the room was told: 'My grandson is going to be a Wallaby.' The nurse had no idea what she was talking about. A few days later that young man and his brother came to say goodbye for the last time. As they made for the door, crumpled with grief, she issued a last command: 'Boys, stand up straight. Now off you go.'

Beneath her Anglican exterior lurked a Presbyterian belief that the day and the hour of all our deaths is set. She had always kept a meticulous diary, a little book that once ruled our lives. No obligation pencilled there, however remote, could ever be shifted. Her notion that death had the same perfect manners seemed to comfort her. They had an appointment. 'When?' she asked as if she wanted to put it in the book. 'When will it happen?' He came at three am. We had been asked to leave her room while she was washed. By the time we returned the fight had entirely gone out of her. I hope some skerrick of consciousness was there at the end to welcome death's arrival on the dot at this conventional hour.

The second funeral was subtly different from the first. People spoke more freely now they were both gone. Nothing remarkable came to light—no scandals, no other families—but we began to learn things we had never known before. What began at the wakes has continued ever since: telling stories about the dead. Fresh facts are welcome as they come along and so are people who have never heard the stories before. But really we tell the old stories because we love telling them. While they are being told, the dead are with us again. And they still have things to tell us about ourselves. 'Pam could never resist showing her hand,' a formidable aunt remarked out of the blue one afternoon. 'We laughed about it for years. She always played the ace too soon.' I'd never heard this killer detail before, absolutely true of her, of me and all of us.

We were never a close family, affectionate but not entangled. Finding ourselves orphans in our forties and fifties meant re-ordering our ties to one another on a basis not defined by our parents: us without them. We ditched the last traces of the roles assigned in childhood. They hadn't been a good fit for a long time yet we had kept playing them while there was still someone left to applaud. That was over. My mother was no longer the clearing house for family news. We had to deal direct. That was a revelation. And we rediscovered each other in the practical business of dismantling our parents' lives and taking responsibility for their property. It was sobering work. Wills make adults of us all. We sent to auction the last bits and pieces no grandchild could be persuaded to take. My mother's uncomfortable chaise longue, her fiercely protected pride and joy, disappeared without attracting a bid. We raised a guilty cheer.

Once both parents are dead their children are supposed to feel in the firing line. I didn't and don't. An older brother's last duty is surely to block the way. What the second death brought was something odd I hadn't expected: a feeling of having grown up at last. Despite the encouragement of many people over many years, I'd thought whatever was possible in that department had happened long ago. Not so. In my mid-fifties, with both parents gone, I felt more adult than I ever had. It's about getting on without them. In nearly every way I had been doing that for a long time. But the backstops were gone. The lines were cut. I was left with what they had given me. As I was puzzling this through, I was struck by something quite unexpected: a sense of growing into them. It's not that I felt any less myself, but who they were was bedding down in me. They haven't taken over. Far from it. But as each year has gone by since they died I find I am more them than I ever was. It's a reassuring surprise. I'm easy in their company.

They died in character. Death is only a transfiguring experience in fiction. We go the way we came. I expect I'll make a noisy exit clamouring for attention. I pray it's not too embarrassing. A good last line would be welcome, some quip to be remembered by. And not a terrible death like theirs, something swift a long way off. Until then I'll tell the grandchildren the old stories, hoping I don't bore them talking about the past, hoping to give them a few clues to themselves and, I suppose, hoping to keep this sweet man and forceful woman alive.

SCRABBLE

MARGARET RICE

The game of Scrabble shaped my mother Jeanette's most enduring relationships. I have an often-repeated memory of Mum sitting in her mother's elegant lounge room, at a card table set up for the purpose of playing this word game. She is with her mother, Irene, who she always referred to as Mother, and one or both of her sisters, Marian and Shirley and someone has said, 'How about a game?'

When any of the four of them got together it was to play Scrabble. Each woman had a set, the tiles made of ivory or wood, and a cup of tea and a chat was only ever a prelude to the real purpose of the day, the game.

So it was no surprise that at three am, twelve hours after we began the most intense phase of our long, laboured deathbed vigil for Mum, someone suggested we play a game in her honour.

We were crowded around her bed in a nursing home in suburban Sydney, so we gently rested the board on her lap and as we did another memory of Mum came back to me.

Mum has just produced a Scrabble bag, along with one of her well-thumbed dictionaries. I am about twelve and our conversation has started airily and I am full of hope. But then I arrange and rearrange my tiles, waiting for inspiration to strike. And no matter what I do, every manoeuvre is leaden and any word power I think I have seems to evaporate.

It would be wonderful to be able to say the dynamic of a game of Scrabble with Mum had changed by the time I reached adulthood. But it never did. Performance anxiety was simply a permanent feature.

I was snapped back to the present by my youngest sister Deb's voice.

'I hated playing Scrabble with Mum,' she muttered and there was a chorus of 'So did I!' from the other four of us in the room and once again we were laughing.

It had been a long and gruelling time, followed by this giddy ride. Twelve hours earlier we were a fraught little assembly— snappy, tense, angry and afraid. Back then I was struggling with a sense that the closer Mum's death got, the more isolated I was from my siblings. But now we were the Rice children again, almost hysterical from a lack of sleep, cabin fever, and awareness of the morbid purpose of our gathering.

Several weeks ago I had taken leave from work to be with Mum as she died, taking the cue from her palliative care specialist, who said she only had three weeks to live. But there had been other whisperings in my ear. Two old friends had urged me to take the time if I could and it had felt like the right thing to do.

But I felt my decision had knocked my relationship with

four of my siblings out of balance, although not that with my intellectually disabled eldest sister, Elizabeth, who would not be able to be at Mum's bedside.

My twin sister, Cecilia, had already organised Elizabeth's last visit to Mum. So I watched as Mum and Elizabeth, both severely incapacitated, nodded at each other and then Elizabeth, hand shaking, passed some flowers to Mum. Knowing this would be their last contact with each other I had cried for both of them.

That left my other two sisters and two brothers. The boys were okay with my decision to spend her last days with Mum. But I seemed to lose the girls.

I had tried to reassure everyone that if I was alone with Mum, I would contact them in enough time for them to to be with her when she died. But my qualifier that it could happen suddenly, without any warning, seemed to unsettle the girls. Nothing was said explicitly but the conversations I had with each of them were edgy. Deb and I got entangled in a frustrating conversation about timelines and Cecilia seemed to withdraw. Nonetheless I pressed on.

I was uncertain what role I would play at the nursing home but I quickly befriended the staff and they answered lots of my questions—except the one that would have helped us the most: *when*.

On my first day I was handed Mum's lunch tray. I took to my task with gusto, forcing her to eat. Powerless, she kept opening her mouth grudgingly, until finally she snarled at me: 'Go away.' I was no longer her daughter but a tormenter and the sneer she gave me was awful.

'Your mum doesn't really need to eat from now on if she doesn't want to,' the sister in charge explained. I didn't know until she said this that eating often stopped some days before death, that this was a sign death was close.

The staff taught me how to wash Mum's eyes, how to readjust her pillow, how to give her hand massages and even how to feed her on the rare occasions she was interested. As the time progressed they let me help them roll Mum over to avoid pressure sores.

At this early point Mum was still conscious, able to ask me about the book I was reading or play with my long string of colourful beads. When she asked for water I gave her sips of thickened cordials which looked like glue; she was losing her swallow reflex and could easily inhale fluids into her lungs. I called the staff when she needed to go to the toilet, ensuring she was never soiled, fed her and as she became more inert and incapable, cleaned her mouth with a refreshing gel on a cotton bud.

The job I loved most was simply holding her hand. If I let it go for a minute she would seek it out again and then smile gently as she wrapped her fingers around mine.

There were times when she leaned in against the side of the bed and rested her head on my shoulders. There were moments when her grip would tighten and I could feel she was afraid. At these moments I would give a gentle squeeze back.

Sometimes I murmured words of comfort: 'It's okay', 'You're not alone' or 'I'm here'. Other times I stroked her forehead. Mostly I said nothing. I knew talk would be tiring and I had learnt the art of silence.

When Mum was asleep I was able to go wandering and exploring through the big old building and its lean-tos. I went down to the laundry to bring up Mum's fresh clothes from her pigeonhole and I organised with the staff there the cleaning of the soft, apricot-coloured negligee and jacket we would lay Mum out in when she died.

Barely touched and still holding the vanilla scent of the cake of soap she had stored it with, it was the set she had worn after our oldest brother, Gerard, was born. He had lived only a few hours but it seemed fitting to bring him back into her story now, as her life ended.

One day I opened a door beside the laundry and found the bay where the recently dead were held—a small room with a high trestle table, the only clue to its purpose the cross on the wall.

But these positive memories of my time with Mum competed with others which were filled with horror.

Mum, a non-smoker, was dying the slow death of lung cancer, more than likely a secondary to breast cancer, although we were never to know for certain.

A lung cancer death is a barbarous one. As the disease progresses, growths in the lung lining fill with fluid, giving the sensation of breathlessness. As Mum's condition deteriorated I spent long days supporting her back while she gasped for breath.

Increasingly Mum developed the look of a wild animal captured in a net. She would grab my arm and ask me to lift her. She would point to her mouth to signal she wasn't getting enough air. I borrowed a hand-held fan and this helped a bit.

But the desire for air would become more urgent as the day wore on and her panic increased as she gasped more and more.

I looked forward to the visits from the others, often in the evenings and I looked forward to the time when we would all be sitting in the room together, sharing our time with Mum.

But my sisters said they wanted to be with Mum by themselves. Deb drew up a roster, splitting our time so we would each be with Mum alone in different sections of the day. I didn't object but in my fragile, exhausted state I felt disappointed.

The roster still left big sheets of time when Mum would need support, so I wasn't worried about not being with her. But I thought this was a sad way to manage what little time was left with her and wished my sisters were happier with a more organic, less structured schedule.

During the next week I tried to grab my bag quickly when one of my sisters arrived. But I always seemed to ask one question too many before regretting it and then fumbling to leave.

I had had more time with Mum than the others but I had not stopped anyone else from being there, yet now I felt judged, felt I was being cast as the controlling big sister. I didn't feel I could have the sensible conversation that might have sorted these jangled emotions, since I was afraid this could lead to conflict at a time when Mum needed peace.

As the time passed and Mum's death loomed, my conversations with Cecilia became shorter and more stilted, so I felt I had lost Cecilia too, normally my closest friend in the world. And as I added a layer of insecurity to my grief, I started to understand that no matter how many siblings you have, ultimately you go through the death of your mother alone.

Besides, there were bigger issues to face. We'd been warned Mum would suffer from agitation and restlessness, more likely with a lung cancer death. But the nursing home staff never seemed to be able to control it, and it continued to worsen. So I lost confidence in their palliative care skills, even though at the same time I wondered whether any medication could have helped Mum.

One night, as the agitation increased, Mum asked me to get a gun. I hoped I had misheard the word.

'Why?' I asked.

'So you can shoot me,' she said.

I asked the night-duty nurse to talk to her, in the hope that she would ramp up the pain relief and a short while later I called Dad in and we sat while I uttered an improvised prayer.

'Dear Lord, please take Mum tonight,' I prayed loudly so she could hear it. There seemed to be little else I could do to help her.

I've since learned the term 'soul pain', used to describe the anguished, existential pain as death approaches. Was this what Mum was suffering from? If so, it seemed to last an inordinately long time.

She had been rejecting prayer now, on the few occasions I or anyone else suggested it. But I wasn't sure whether this was because she preferred to say her own, or if it was a rejection of religion or a rejection of God. Would more faith in God have eased this? Or more preparedness to talk about death in the years before? Or was she struggling against the cold, hard emptiness of the grave, no matter what her religious beliefs were?

As I watched her face now, I felt I saw what she was afraid of, felt my own face pressed in against tightly packed earth and my own body disintegrating.

A few days later oxygen helped Mum to sink into an exhausted rest and I left that night thinking I would at last get a good night's sleep. But I didn't sleep at all, haunted by the image of Mum struggling for breath. In my sleep I felt her weight on my shoulders as I tried to lift her while she struggled for air and it became a recurring nightmare.

I walked into the room the next morning to find her sitting on the edge of her bed, her oxygen mask flung off, repeating her now constant refrain, 'I want to go home.'

As a young woman Mum had written poetry and she had taken it up again when her family left home. We started reading Mum's poetry to her separately and together in the evenings, when the roster had finished and this seemed to comfort her.

In the quiet of her room as she lay dying, her work seemed to come into its own and her poems now seemed to blossom into their true meaning. What in a previous time might have seemed mawkish to me now was deeply moving.

The last day she was conscious, while sitting up in bed, she leaned in against my side and began to play with my long beads. I started to take them off to give to her and she whispered, 'No.' So what she'd liked about them was their attachment to me? I clung to this thought.

And as she shut her eyes, now struggling to squeeze the last measure of oxygen out of each breath, I read one of her poems to her again, tears welling up in me.

Seek not to still the hours of day
Lest you in vain, hold not, but drive away
This fleeting time . . .

For a second she seemed to stop struggling and recognising the words, she turned and smiled and with a sense of horror I realised it was probably one of the last times she would acknowledge me.

'Mum, I wish I'd appreciated your poetry more,' I said through my tears.

Had I discussed her poems enough with her? Why hadn't I shrugged off my childish embarrassment over my perception that Mum was an amateur and asked her about the meaning behind each one, the places she was when she wrote them, the people who had inspired them?

'Just as you're going, I want to grab this important part of you,' I sobbed as she appeared to turn towards me then sank back onto the bed.

It turned out I was right. Mum would never 'see' me again. My regret about not appreciating her more, wishing I could have one more encounter with her, eventually eased. But the sense that I had been able to give everything I could to her in those last few days was to remain and I understood all that she had given me in a way I hadn't before. So I could let her go now.

During this time, Dad would visit for short periods throughout the day. Often I'd arrive during one of his earlier visits and I would be there at night. Still feeling isolated from my sisters and reproached by a throwaway comment, I asked him if I was inhibiting his visits to Mum. He said emphatically: 'No, you are my sword and my buckler.'

We agreed he'd be frank when he wanted me to leave and I was always careful to ask if he wanted me to go, often timing a coffee break around his visits.

In the days before she lost consciousness, as soon as Mum heard his voice it seemed to calm her. No matter who was in the room, like a teenage girl, she would pucker up to him and pull him in for long, smooching kisses.

Dad and I would often finish these days with dinner together.

'I'm finding those kisses a bit confronting,' he confessed at one of these meals.

'She seems to be winding the clock back,' I volunteered.

After Mum lost consciousness she was just an automaton. She continued the cycle of bracing herself and sitting up but it was a rhythmic reflex action, almost an involuntary response—the person behind it gone.

Eventually the roster was abandoned and one day I said to Mum when Deb turned up: 'Here's your baby Debbie.'

Then, worried Deb would be offended by the baby reference, I mumbled an apology.

'No, I don't mind it at all; I *am* her baby,' she said.

At that moment I understood her better. There was a year between Elizabeth and the twins, Cecilia and me. Julian was born two years after us, Damian sixteen months later and then three and a half years after that Deb arrived. The top end of the family were babies together.

In taking time off work I had returned to my childhood role as Mum's little helper. Deb was also replicating her early childhood but it was very different from mine. As a toddler she was alone with Mum while the rest of us were at school.

The following Saturday I decided to stay away from the nursing home, knowing there would be others visiting. When I did arrive there was a crisis as Mum's breathing became very erratic, speeding up then slowing down, followed by what seemed an eternity with no breathing at all.

Julian had left Sydney three years earlier to make a new life for himself and his young family in Tamworth but he was coming down every weekend to be with Mum before she died. He was with me at her bedside as we waited for Cecilia and Dad to arrive.

'Can you see what I see?' I asked Julian.

'Yes, what does it mean?' he replied.

I had heard of Cheyne-Stokes respiration and realised this abnormal breathing was it. I wondered if it meant Mum would die that night.

'Should I ring the others?' I asked Julian.

'Yes,' he said.

I rang Damian and Deb, conscious that it might be a false alarm. It was but they were nonetheless glad I'd called.

'I'd rather be contacted than not,' Deb said.

That night Mum was the most responsive she had been for forty-eight hours. As Deb talked to her she sat up and leaned her head in slowly to touch Deb's.

It was an extraordinary moment, as though Mum were being drawn to something light and magnetic. And then I realised she was. Deb is a beautiful blonde. Enthralled by Mum, I no longer saw Deb as the powerful, successful career woman that she is but as a vulnerable child who needed her mother one more time.

Something Deb had said the week before came back to me, something I'd dismissed without accepting, which I now did.

'Mum was a different mother to all of us,' she had said.

Deb was right. Mum had revealed such different relationships with each of us, particularly during the last few weeks. But most importantly, there was a place for us all.

Seeing these differences and aware of Deb's vulnerability, I wanted to show Deb I had never meant to be a threat, that if I had been it had been unintended. So later that night I sat Deb on my knee where Mum could see her and she could see Mum. Deb did not scoff at or dismiss me but seemed to appreciate the gesture.

Realising it was Mum's last weekend, Julian said goodbye to us and explained he probably wouldn't be back before Mum died. As a teacher, he had commitments the following week, the end of the school year, and he expected Mum's dying would all be over by the time he was finished.

Over the next two days, Mum's condition deteriorated further and we settled in for her death vigil but we had the overwhelming sense she was waiting for someone. On Tuesday night I rang Julian in Tamworth.

Was it some powerful family force that was keeping him away, maybe oppressive big-sister energy, I asked.

'Nah, just school commitments,' he said.

'Then come, we need you. It might not make much difference to her now but we think she's waiting for you,' I said.

He decided that as soon as he had finished his last lesson the next day his family would head down to Sydney.

Just at the time we knew Julian was leaving Tamworth on the Wednesday, Mum seemed to have a bad turn. She developed a loud death rattle and despite being unconscious she looked frightened and as though she was in real pain. Extra morphine was administered.

Each one of us struggled in our fear and anxiety to hold Mum's hand, each one of us wanting to comfort her, each one of us a frightened, fragile child.

A short while later Dad picked up *The Pageant of English Poetry* and read Elizabeth Barrett Browning's 'How do I love thee? Let me count the ways'. I was awestruck. For a moment Mum and Dad were young again, they were lovers. And clearly it was a poem he had read to her a thousand times before. Reading this poem was his goodbye and Mum seemed to know it, seemed to turn a little closer in towards Dad as he recited it.

Suddenly I understood what all Mum's puckering up to Dad over recent weeks had been about. She was showing us he was her lover, that whatever the trials and tribulations of their long marriage, this was the most powerful relationship in the room and it always had been.

Later that night Dad decided not to stay with Mum while she died, and he left. They had already said their goodbyes. Somehow, we knew that Mum was reconciled to this and just as she had given birth without him, she would die without him being present.

We continued to sit, waiting for Julian and over the next few hours the expression on Mum's face finally seemed to move from the anguish and terror of the last few weeks to a look of acceptance.

About midnight Julian walked in the door, wearing a wide-brimmed rain hat. He looked every bit the country boy. He grabbed Mum's hand and kissed it. Her mouth was now locked open, in the way of the dying so close to death. He slipped into place as though he had been with us all day.

We are a Catholic family and, although not a particularly devout one, we thought maybe it was time to recite a decade of the rosary.

'I'll never forget when I went to Aunty Rita's for a holiday and she sprung me for not knowing the rosary,' Damian recalled.

'After the words "Hail Mary" I started guessing and instead of saying "Hail Mary, full of grace" I said, "Hail Mary, full of oranges". I spent the next two weeks doing Hail Mary training. She wasn't going to let me go home until I knew it.'

I was not surprised that structured prayer hadn't worked for us and that it didn't release Mum to go. But we had started to loosen up and instead of hiding our insecurities we were starting to share them, causing much hilarity.

Cecilia's usual self-deprecating humour returned. She told us Mum had asked her just a couple of days ago, 'Are there only just the two of us here?' When Cecilia leaned in to her and said, 'Yes', Mum replied, 'That's no good.'

Cecilia was crestfallen but, as Mum rambled on, she realised that Mum was back in the nursing ward where she was in charge nearly sixty years earlier. She thought Cecilia was another nurse and there weren't enough on duty for them to do their rounds.

We were in full reminiscence mode now and we moved from the sacred to the profane and told a round of her favourite dirty jokes. But still she seemed no closer to death.

By one am Mum was warm and her fingers and toes had lost their distinct blue hue. When I felt her forehead it was clammy and when I pointed this out to the others they looked frightened. Instead of cooling down she was warming up.

'I think she's got pneumonia,' I said.

It was the only explanation for the strange reversal coming over her. Otherwise, how would this play out? Would she come back to life and forget about this dying business? This could only lead to another torturous descent towards death, a repulsive thought, since there was only so much agonised dying one woman could be expected to do.

Whatever the explanation, it was clear we would be here all night. We needed something to help us through it.

And it was then that we thought of the Scrabble, fossicking around in a drawer for the set.

When we found five tile holders the hairs on the back of my neck stood on end.

We nestled in beside her and began to play, invoking her help when we couldn't get a word or needed her inspiration to improve our score.

There was an eerie quality to the game, right from the very beginning.

I could see something of our lives in the words we laid out. There was 'sepia' from Deb, who had a passion for old family photos. Damian put out 'gay', opening up a triple word score for someone else, and 'tout' went out early, one in the cluster of names of a law firm Cecilia had once worked for. And soon 'ta' was there, the only word Mum ever used to say thank you.

The game was intense. I tried to persuade everyone 'ib' was a word but failed miserably. Damian started to add 'oo' to a 'c' but Cecilia pointed to a 'z' and so he improved his score. I put out 'slave', which soon became 'enslaved'—I was enslaved by my insecurities.

As usual, Deb and I went in hard, playing to win. After the second round I had the early lead. By the third round we were equal. But then I slipped further and further behind and as I did I felt the strong sensation that I was falling—not surprising on little sleep and at three-thirty am. Yet it was as though Mum were whispering in my ear, 'She will win but let go, it's okay.'

And as the game continued the message changed to: 'Life is just a game, don't take it so seriously. Yes, work hard but build good relationships and have some fun too.'

By the end of the game we had a new maturity and a new easy communication. Or was it simply that Mum had reeled us back to a much earlier time, when we were innocent children, all goofing around together?

The game finished at about four am and we settled down to sleep, exhausted, falling onto blankets and rugs the night staff had gathered for us.

Dad walked in at about seven-thirty, bewildered that Mum was still alive.

'Breakfast anyone?' he asked and the six of us strolled down the street for bacon and eggs at a local coffee shop.

As we walked we fell into clusters of two and sometimes three, chatting and laughing, easily moving from one person to another within the group. When we pulled the coffee shop tables together Deb said, 'Hey, notice something? Any configuration we sit in works.'

We were now six people working perfectly well together. We were in perfect balance. We didn't need Mum to make things work any more; we could finally let her go.

I had the overwhelming sense that this was the moment Mum had been waiting for. She'd brought us together but not until each one of us had worked out how to be alone.

When we came back from breakfast Mum was still alive but failing rapidly. While Cecilia and I were outside the room, distracted and still getting organised, Julian told Mum she could go. Later Damian and Deb said he was emphatic yet gentle as he held her.

'You can do it, you can do it,' he had said.

When Cecilia and I came into the room Mum's breathing was very erratic. While the others drew in close I sat back. There was only room for four and she had given me all I needed.

Over the next ten minutes we watched as her breathing gradually stopped, not a clear-cut moment but simply defined by the absence of the next breath. Mum had finally died.

The women in the family, including Julian's wife Marie, who we now invited to join us, washed Mum's body and we were able to say our last goodbyes. In her apricot negligee she looked beautiful and finally at peace.

Later that day I talked to Julian about his role.

With a grin on his face he told me: 'You know how Mum always loved a good pun? Well let me tell you a little story.' His eye teeth showed, always a sign that mischief was coming.

'She knew I was living in the country and I'm planning to get goats for our property. When I was sitting with her last

Sunday I told her. So, you see, I am the goat-whisperer. But she misunderstood; she thought I said I was the ghost-whisperer,' he said, chuckling.

That night I had my usual dream: Mum was tightly coiled around me. But in my dream I was surrounded by a white light and then I was woken by intense nausea. As I sat up in bed to settle myself I noticed that outside a violent storm was raging. Next I had the sense Mum was being unfurled from me then pulled up into the storm and whisked away. For the first time in three weeks I felt free.

Over the next weekend we sat in a circle of six, five children and Dad, three women and three men, planning Mum's funeral and working in what seemed to be perfect harmony.

The intense accord Mum had seemed to fashion during our Scrabble game started to loosen once her funeral was over and we began to go our separate ways. But I had new insights into my siblings and a new trust.

Less than eight weeks later our beloved Julian, self-dubbed goat-whisperer, was also dead, killed in a motorbike accident. We came together again to plan a funeral. But this one brought with it a sense of violation and tragedy, of lives torn apart, not somehow brought to completion; of harmony destroyed, of balance ripped asunder.

I look back on that strange morning, when we all walked together and the easy way we were with each other over breakfast the day Mum died and I realise it was a brief, shining, magical moment.

For we will never, ever be in that formation of six again.

GOODBYE, PORKPIE HAT:
16 WAYS TO SAY FAREWELL

MANDY SAYER

1

HE'D BEEN DEAD TWELVE YEARS, but he was still in my hands. The prints were faded, the edges frilled with light. The week before I'd found my father's old camera in a kitchen cupboard, with a roll of film still inside. I'd dropped it off at a local shop and an hour later had picked up the prints. In one photo he's sitting in a Sydney pub, a schooner of beer in one hand, cigarette in the other. He's wearing a T-shirt from New Orleans, printed with *Always for Pleasure* in gold, and staring directly at the lens with a wicked grin, as if he were about to tell me a dirty joke. I flicked through the other shots: Gerry in his late seventies, wearing cowboy boots, dancing in an unfamiliar park. Gerry practising drums in his one-room flat. Gerry with his eyes closed, sitting beside a sunflower, smoking a joint in a friend's backyard.

He was the first to go; my mother went five years later. While he did not go gentle into that good night, she went passively—even deliberately—once she could no longer walk up the stairs to her bedroom or shuffle to the front gate on her Zimmer frame.

Her final message to me is still on the answering machine. I can tell by the curl in her voice that she's had a few drinks, but is not yet completely gone. Nothing special. Just the usual, *Hi, it's Mum here.* Maybe she didn't know she was about to die, or maybe she didn't care.

I later learned that, as she was being loaded into an ambulance, my younger brother squeezed her hand and said, *I love you, Mum.*

He didn't know it at the time, but she was about to utter her last words. Not, *I love you, too*, or, *Take care of yourself.*

She looked into his eyes and replied, *I know.*

2

In July 1999, he was given six months to live. The tumour in his left lung was bigger than a walnut. He wasn't disappointed, he was furious, stomping out of the doctor's surgery and yelling, to no one in particular, *Fucking cigarettes!* He was by then almost eighty and had been smoking, on and off, since he was a teenager. The jazz drummer's life certainly hadn't helped: long nights, booze and drugs, skipping meals, a fag for breakfast.

I moved him into my one-bedroom apartment in Kings Cross, into the queen-sized bed with harbour views, while I slept on the floor in the living room. I'd been divorced only sixteen months and was still recovering from a decade-long marriage.

By this time my father was coughing up blood every few minutes and spitting it into a plastic bucket. He'd escaped death many, many times before, having survived being born, in 1920, with a hare lip and cleft palate. He'd also endured numerous operations, a near-fatal car crash at the age of forty-eight, a heart attack and triple bypass at sixty-eight and, at seventy, a deadly melanoma so close to his brain a laser surgeon had to be flown in from the US in order to remove it.

In spite of the doctor's diagnosis of terminal cancer, Gerry kept praying—literally—for a miracle, saying the rosary every morning after he'd taken his pills. He still had lots of things to do—starting a funk band, harvesting his three mature marijuana plants, learning to windsurf—and this dying business was slowing him down.

He'd grow cranky over the slightest inconvenience: being served tepid tea, the number of ads on TV, not being able to have a shit after breakfast. The only things that would restore his good cheer were a blood transfusion and an enema, in that order. After which time he'd sip a glass of red wine and brag about where he planned to tour his funk band the following year.

3

The hardest part is not the death itself, but when you're confronted with a museum of relics, a conservatory of junk that no one else could ever love. It usually happens after the funeral, after the mountains of paperwork are completed, after the flowers stop arriving and everyone has gone home.

On opening the front door of my mother's housing department home, the first thing I spotted was the yellow glass ashtray beside her lounge chair, filled with the butts of her final cigarettes, the ones that eventually killed her.

The paraphernalia dotting the top of a cabinet: dusty ceramic frogs; a Chinese doll; a figurine of a shoeless boy sitting on a stump, fishing; eggs painted with miniature landscapes mounted inside plastic cubes. The curtains, once white, now smoked to the colour of drizzling rain. In the laundry, a pair of knickers soaking in a bucket of stagnant water.

A frilly doily of a bedroom: a nylon lace eiderdown and matching bedhead, a lampshade threaded with ribbons, a framed picture on the wall of a downcast kitten with Betty Boop eyes. Her wardrobe filled with elasticised trousers and cardigans bought from St Vincent de Paul.

Underneath the stairs: a shopping trolley, a Zimmer frame, a walking stick that I gave her as a joke, with a retractable handle that held a secret whisky flask. The balls of used tissues beneath the cushion on her chair. A spice rack on the wall, not filled with oregano and thyme, but with Serepax, Atenolol, Valium, Nicardipin, Panamax and Mogadon. Under the kitchen sink, an enamel bowl with years of accumulated dripping inside, flecked with bacon bits.

It's a part of the process no one else ever witnesses, not the doctor, not the funeral director, not the priest, certainly not the close friends: the pilled sheets on the bed, the spare asthma puffer in the drawer, the set of false teeth floating in a cloudy glass of water on the crooked bathroom shelf.

As I looked at them I realised that one day somebody would be faced with my own gallery of private things, significant to no one but the person I'd once been. How would that somebody feel about finding a lock of blond hair in a ceramic pillbox? Or discovering a drawer full of defunct vibrators? Or the storage baskets under the sink in my bathroom, holding extra plastic shower curtain rings, loose emery boards, empty skin cream jars, tins of hardened shoe polish, a laminated student ID card from 1980 of a swollen-faced girl, wearing one earring, with circles under her eyes.

4

When my maternal grandmother died from a heart attack at the age of eighty-four, Mum was so bereft she sat on the couch for a week, drinking brandy and weeping—so much so that she was unable to fly from Melbourne to Sydney in order to attend the funeral. They'd been unusually close, especially after my mother's father had deserted the family when she was seven years old and run off to Tasmania with a woman he'd met at the general post office.

The image of her handsome father, my mother formed an unnaturally close bond with her own mother, Dolly, who favoured her over the other three children. And, like Dolly, my mother had spent most of her life chasing men who were either unavailable or incapable of unselfish love.

Only months before Mum died, I put an ad in the paper, in search of my lost grandfather or his relatives. I waited and waited, and so did she, but there was never a response.

Even at the end of her life, she still yearned to be loved by the first man who'd deserted her, seventy years before.

5

On my father's seventy-ninth birthday—which we both knew would be his last—I walked him through Darlinghurst to his usual radiotherapy session at St Vincent's Hospital. As he swept into the clinic, he playfully announced to the staff and others in the waiting room, *Now why is it called radiotherapy when there's no radio playing? How are we supposed to get better without any music?*

The nurses laughed and a woman hooked up to an oxygen machine nodded, arching her eyebrows.

Later, back at home, Gerry wasn't so irreverent. I'd invited a few friends around for a little party but a pain had begun to stab him in the stomach and he told me to cancel it. The pain grew worse; I put the bottles of wine back on top of the fridge. Half an hour later, he was doubled over.

I called his doctor, who faxed through a prescription for morphine. Desperate to make him comfortable for this one last birthday, I ran through Kings Cross to the chemist across the road from the El Alamein Fountain with the prescription in my hand. The bald pharmacist, who'd worked in the Cross for over thirty years, took one look at what had been prescribed and shook his head. *We don't keep this stuff on the premises any more. The junkies always hold us up and steal it.*

I tried the chemist further down, then the one near the railway station, and then the one across the road, where my friend Hughie the drag queen worked behind the counter. That night he was wearing a pink and white gingham fifties dress and a blonde wig. Hughie, too, smiled and shook his head. *No one in the Cross keeps morphine these days.*

I thought of my father lying on the couch, twisting in pain, unable to walk or eat. *Please, Hughie*, I begged. *It's my dad's birthday.*

Hughie raised one long red fingernail to his lips and tapped them, as if punching data into a machine. *Well, you could try Taylor Square. They're open twenty-four hours. Tell Bert that I sent you.*

An hour later I was in my living room, measuring the bitter-smelling syrup into a medicine cup. By this time Gerry had recovered slightly, having managed, in my absence, to open one of the bottles of red wine and fill a tumbler each for us. I handed him the cup and he downed the contents in one gulp. He paused, took a sip of wine, then grabbed the bottle of morphine from my hand and took another long swig, as if it were a chaser.

I think it's working! he announced, his eyes suddenly bright.

I sat opposite him, relieved, and kicked off my shoes.

Why don't you have a hit? he suggested, holding up the brown bottle. *You look a bit uptight.*

Nah, I'm all right. I picked up my tumbler and raised it to him. *Cheers*, I said, and took a sip.

No, go on! he insisted.

I shook my head. *I'm happy with the wine.*

He slid to the edge of his seat. *You'll get a nice buzz*, he cajoled. *C'mon, it's my birthday. Let's get high together!*

I looked at his sunken face, the pale, ice-blue eyes, and realised that, by this time next year, he'd be gone forever. The idea was preposterous—him not being around—as impossible as oxygen suddenly vanishing from the air.

He proffered the brown bottle again and this time I accepted it. As I took the first gulp, I baulked: it tasted like lighter fluid.

But I kept drinking it down so I could also swallow the sob rising in my throat.

6

The day my father lost his own mother he was rehearsing with his six-piece jazz band in the living room. By this time, in the early sixties, he'd been married twelve years and he and my mother had had two kids.

She was in the kitchen when the telegram arrived: *Mum died this morning. Love, Joan.*

Unfortunately, both my mother and father had sisters named Joan and she immediately began weeping, presuming her own mother had died. She banged on the living room door, summoning him. Then she noticed the postmark on the telegram, *Wollongong*, and realised it was Gerry's family who'd sent it.

My father opened the door and breezed into the kitchen. *Yeah, Bet?* he asked. *What's up?*

This just arrived. She handed him the message. *Thank God it's your mother and not mine—*

The words were barely out of her mouth before she regretted having uttered them. But my father took no offence at all, just glanced at the telegram and shrugged. There were five men in the next room and they were in the middle of an important concert rehearsal. He handed the missive back to my mother. *Oh, well*, he said, *she was old anyway.*

He turned and walked back towards his kit of drums, slamming the door behind him.

7

Within months of his diagnosis, my father grew thin and gaunt, refused to bathe, and barked at me relentlessly. He complained of a knifing pain in his chest and, after I took him into the emergency ward again for treatment, he was admitted to St Vincent's Hospice.

It was during this period that I asked a friend if he would shoot some video footage of my father. Louis and I had been editing a book together that year and he was the only person I knew who owned a camera. Gerry was fading away, from the world, from his own life, and from me. I was already missing him, and wanted to create a keepsake.

Gerry was wary of Louis at first, as he was of any man who might compete for his daughter's attention. But as the filming progressed, Louis slowly won him over with his humour and lack of guile. Gerry was impressed by Louis's snappy suits and snakeskin boots, and by his habit of always turning up to these sessions with a bottle of gin. By the third afternoon of shooting, we three were like a trio of old raconteurs, sipping martinis on the balcony of the hospice and trading stories. Sometimes Gerry would demand that I roll him a joint, which I did, and we'd share it as Louis continued shooting.

I'd put him to bed at eight o'clock, kiss him goodnight, and turn out the light. That was always the hardest time: closing the door and leaving him behind, not knowing if he'd still be alive when I returned in the morning. Louis would walk me home, his slender arm wrapped around me, as if I were too young or confused to cross a busy city street on my own.

8

My mother deliberately smoked herself to death. She'd been warned, many times, that she would die if she continued, but by the age of seventy-three she'd decided she'd had enough.

During one of our last telephone conversations, she was drunk, complaining that she was lonely, even though my thirty-year-old half-brother still lived at home in order to care for her.

Throughout my adult life, she'd pressured me to have children, particularly during the early, happy years of my first marriage, but by the time she was dying, all that had changed.

Don't bother having kids, she exhorted. I could hear the clink of ice against glass as she took a sip of something—probably brandy. *It's a waste of time. You spend your whole life looking after them and what do you get in return? A bloody card at Christmas!*

9

Don't bother about a funeral for me, my mother always joked. *When the time comes, just put me in a garbage bag and chuck me over the cemetery fence!*

When I miss her I like to wear her clothes—or, more precisely, her knee-length pink nighties. I flounce around my apartment in them, dancing to Benny Goodman.

And nearly a decade after her death, I still keep a tube of her lipstick, also pink, in my makeup bag. It looked better on her than it does on me, but every now and then I like to press it to my lips and taste her once again.

10

Cleaning out his studio apartment was more difficult than watching him die. He hadn't lived in it for many months, preferring either to stay with me, or to have some respite in St Vincent's Hospice.

When it came time to sort out his stuff, clean the studio, and return the keys to the Department of Housing, he'd been dead five weeks. Yet walking into his flat, it seemed as if he'd just popped down to the pub to pick up a six-pack of beer or have a flutter on the races. A little like those scenes from Pompeii, with a single, inconsequential moment from daily life preserved in ash: the saucer on the coffee table, knotted with roaches from his final joints; a racing guide with numbers scrawled in the margins; crockery and utensils on the sideboard, mostly stolen from pubs and clubs: glazed, white Irish coffee mugs, schooner glasses printed with AHA; a dinner plate from the City of Sydney RSL, another from Royal North Shore Hospital. On the wall hung last year's calendar, advertising his local pharmacy, with crosses and circles in certain squares, probably indicating his wins and losses at the racetrack months before. I opened the spare fridge and found piles of sheet music stacked inside, his treasured private library. Under the sink, a bong made out of an Orchy bottle, still half filled with loamy water.

The only thing of any worth he owned was his kit of drums, fully set up in the middle of the room, the skins and cymbals covered with blankets to keep the dust off.

In the wardrobe, not much, mostly clothes borrowed from other people and never returned: a couple of my old T-shirts and jumpers, one of my leather jackets, some trackie daks. A three-piece cream and tan suit that, for the past twenty-five years, he'd worn on special occasions. I could still smell his scent, like cooked oatmeal. I lifted the waistcoat and pressed it to my face, inhaling him one last time.

11

Gerry survived the first stroke. When he regained consciousness, after a twelve-hour coma, I realised his personality had changed yet again, and the sweet and genial man I had known all my life returned threefold. He was calm and affectionate. He began smoking cigars and his sense of humour ran riot. When the hospital barber entered his shared ward and asked if anyone needed a haircut, Gerry retorted, in his loudest voice, *I'll have a shampoo and a blow job!* When he saw a fellow patient whom he loathed kissing the resident cat on the mouth, he declared with great glee, *Do you know that just five minutes ago that cat was licking its arse?* The doctor explained to me that the stroke had performed a minor lobotomy on his frontal lobe, essentially zapping out his aggressive behaviour. Sometimes, in the afternoons, he'd leave the hospice, wearing my purple satin pyjamas, and walk down the street to the Darlo Bar, where he'd sink a few schooners and hold court with the local bar flies.

He was released from the hospice between Christmas and New Year's Eve, 1999, painfully thin, yet optimistic. He had so little weight on him that, as I was unlocking the door to my building, a blast of wind blew him over.

12

My mother's funeral was held in a Catholic church, presided over by a priest named Father Fortunato, who clearly didn't enjoy his work. During the arrangements, two days prior, he enlisted my sister and me to read most of the prayers and lead every one of the hymns. At first, I thought his strategy was a compassionate one, insisting that the relatives of the deceased conduct the ceremony themselves to help them quell their grief. But once the actual funeral began, I realised he was not only uninterested, he was clearly bored. He sat to the side of the pulpit, head bowed, occasionally glancing at his watch, and when he did speak briefly he mumbled so much no one could figure out if he were reciting 'Hail Mary' or 'Mary Had a Little Lamb'.

Towards the conclusion of the ceremony, when my sister went to sing a final song, 'God Bless the Child', he waved a hand, cut her off, and gestured to the coffin bearers to carry my mother away, which we did, lifting the casket to our shoulders and hurrying obediently down the aisle.

Later, outside the church, as people milled about kissing and hugging, Father Fortunato emerged from the depths of the church and looked around, squinting against the glare. I watched him spot me and then make a beeline towards the hearse, beside which I was standing. He paused, hugged me, saying he was sorry for my loss. And then he admired the black lace dress I was wearing.

What are you doing later? he asked, stroking me on the cheek. *I have some lovely red wine back in the rectory, if you like, to help you with your grief.*

13

One morning in early January 2000, as I was handing my father his morning medication, his body stiffened, his eyes rolled back and he fell into my arms, trembling violently, as if he were having an epileptic fit.

I rode with him in the ambulance and, after he was admitted to emergency, I was taken to a small room and informed by a doctor that he'd had a second, more serious stroke and could die at any time. I had him transferred to the hospice, where I knew he would receive the medication and care that would allow him to pass away as painlessly as possible.

When Gerry regained consciousness, it was obvious even to him that he had very little time left. He'd lost his motor coordination and was now unable to feed himself or go to the bathroom, though he was able to hold a glass of wine in his trembling hands, to raise it to his mouth.

For a long time he held my free hand, repeatedly lifting it to his lips and kissing my fingers, my knuckles, over and over.

Yes, Gerry, I said, *there's not enough kissing in the world.*

No, he replied, glancing directly at me, *there's not enough fucking in the world.*

It was the last lucid comment he would ever make.

Now, my father would always be unavailable to me, and the greatest distance of them all would forever circumscribe our relationship. Louis had videotaped part of Gerry's final hours, how he'd wheezed into an oxygen mask, the way he'd held my hand and gazed at me sorrowfully with glazed blue eyes. Hours later, after Gerry had fallen into a coma, a nurse wheeled in a foldout bed for me so I could sleep beside him through the night. When I awoke at one am, a nurse told me he'd passed away ten minutes earlier.

As I stood beside his bed I noticed his eyes were still open and staring at the ceiling. I touched one lid and pressed it down, but it automatically popped open again, as if winking back at me.

14

His funeral was on a warm, sunny day in the middle of summer. I organised a five-piece jazz band to play in the church, which was packed with musicians, actors, bar flies and relatives. Whenever anyone stood up to tell a story about Gerry, they always apologised first to the Catholic priest, because Gerry obviously swore a lot and to imitate him truthfully one had to utter a lot of *fucks!*

Father Murphy, however, thought it was all hilarious good fun, and every time the band played a song or someone told yet another funny story, I'd see him nick out the side of the pulpit and guzzle on a goblet of wine, after which he'd reappear with an even darker red circle rimming his lips.

By this time, the singing had attracted the elderly nuns from the college next door, who stood at the back of the church, both mesmerised and shocked. Mesmerised, because listening to Jeff Duff crooning the song 'In Space, Everybody Jams with Miles' was pure and transcendental bliss; shocked, because the song defines the late jazz trumpeter, Miles Davis, as the one and only true God: *If you want to jam with John Coltrane, you've got to ask the man . . . You can hear them playing up in heaven, playing in Miles' Saintly All-Star Band . . .*

The nuns later told me that if a bishop had happened to turn up, poor old Father Murphy would have been disrobed and kicked out of the Church altogether for encouraging blasphemy.

After we carried the coffin out to the hearse, the band and congregation filed out and followed it down Darlinghurst Road—which the police had closed off—all playing percussion instruments in time with the saxophonist's fast blues. The hearse turned left into Liverpool Street and everyone repaired to the Darlo Bar for the wake.

Inside, with a drink in her hand, my mother performed the role of the bereaved widow well, even though she and my father had been separated for over twenty-seven years and she now had an adult son fathered by another man. She howled against the chests of my father's old friends, some of whom she'd had flings with decades before. When a fight between my brothers threatened to derail the evening, I invited friends back to my apartment and asked Louis if he could walk my tipsy mother back to my place. He later told me she'd flirted with him in the lift and, as he guided her towards my front door, she turned and leaned against him. *Don't get involved with Mandy*, she warned. *She's very promiscuous.*

15

You've got to stop writing about your father so much, my mother admonished, again on the phone. *It's like you're obsessed or something.*

I could tell by the higher pitch of her voice that she'd already drunk three or four beers. Tipsy enough to want to voice her opinions; still sober enough to articulate them.

Two days before, my memoir *Dreamtime Alice* had been named the winner of the 2000 National Biography Award. The book was based on the three years Gerry and I had spent performing on the streets together in the US—he drumming, me tap dancing—and even though the win was a pleasant surprise, it was also painful to realise that I wouldn't be able to share the experience with him. Bereft, I wore his three-piece suit and tie to the award ceremony at the New South Wales State Library and of course mentioned him in my acceptance speech. The following day, a half-page picture of me in his suit, and quotes from my speech, ended up on page three of the Saturday papers.

Every interview you give, my mother continued. *Every newspaper article. You can't stop talking about your father. It's ridiculous!*

I could hear her dragging heavily on a cigarette and pictured her blowing smoke out the side of her mouth.

For fuck's sake, Mum, I said. *Give me a break. He's only been dead for eight weeks.*

16

One day, long before he got sick, we were sitting on my veranda overlooking Kings Cross, listening to a recording of the jazz musician Charles Mingus, when my father asked me, *Do you know the story behind this tune?*

I sipped my beer and listened. I recognised the melody but couldn't name the song—a slow, moody ballad with lots of backing horns.

Gerry didn't wait for me to answer. *Well, one night in the late fifties, Mingus was onstage in a New York club, playing the piano, when a bloke crept up to him and whispered in his ear that Prez had died.*

I looked up quizzically, wondering who he was talking about.

You know—Prez, prompted Gerry. *Lester Young, the sax player. He always wore that funny hat.*

I recalled Young's heartbreaking collaborations with Billie Holiday, and nodded. I also remembered the funny hat Gerry was referring to—a grey, floppy thing with a crooked brim.

So Mingus, Gerry continued, *he was a huge fan of Prez, so when he heard he'd just died, you know what he did?*

I gulped at my beer again and shook my head.

Well, he was so upset he couldn't stop playing the piano. But instead of going on with the tune they were in the middle of, Mingus segued into a piece of music no one had heard before.

Over my father's voice I listened to the trumpets and trombone soaring through the speakers, a shout and chant of longing.

Gerry drained his can and dropped it on the ground. *You see, the tempo slowed right down and the rest of the band had to listen hard so that they could pick up the changes.* He slid to the edge of his chair, grinning. Sunlight angled through the leaves of a plane tree across the street and he closed his eyes against the glare.

But what they didn't know, he continued, *was that Mingus was inventing the tune as he went along—he was improvising, you know—he was composing his farewell, moment by moment.*

Gerry's eyes suddenly snapped open and he leaned into a shadow. *And you know what Mingus called the tune?*

I shook my head.

He called it, 'Goodbye, Porkpie Hat'.

I glanced at my father, at his helmet of thick blond hair, his scarred lips and crooked nose, and wanted to remain sitting in the sun, in this moment with him, forever.

DISBELIEF

SUSAN WYNDHAM

IN THE DAYS AND WEEKS AFTER my mother's death, my husband explained to anyone who asked that she had died at home, in her own bed, in her sleep and with her daughter by her side. A good death, a peaceful death, he implied, the kind people hope for. They were comforting words, which I did not begrudge, and they were almost true. But every time I heard them I wanted to say, 'No, no, it wasn't that simple.'

It was just the two of us that last night as it had been, in some ways, all my life, and I am haunted by the things I did not do, the things I should have said. I see her falling in slow motion, over and over and over, and wonder how I might have caught her. I cannot believe she is gone.

My mother went to hospital twice in her life. The first time was to have me in 1957, a slow, smooth birth that she recalled with unfaded bliss on my birthday every year while I listened with a tight smile of adolescent embarrassment, even in my fifties. The intensity of her love was a raft that buoyed me and a responsibility that sometimes, I'm ashamed to say, weighed me down.

Among her papers after her death I found a recent note headed *Important Memories*. Second on the list, in her lively handwriting, was *Seeing & holding my baby daughter immediately after birth. Violet blue eyes, long black hair, dear little face. 8lbs 2ozs. Born 9pm. Sandwiches & tea (yum). Next morning nurses brought Susie in with pink ribbon tying up her hair. Oh joy!*

I smiled and cried at the familiar details. Darling, devoted Mum. What the note left out was the miserable background to her newborn joy. When she left hospital—when we left— her ten-year marriage to my father was collapsing and she was already a single mother. Dad was more than halfway out the door, in love with the woman who would become his second wife, when I was conceived. It was the last time they had sex, Mum told me much later. Whenever I suggested her life would have been easier without me, she was emphatic: 'You are the best thing that ever happened to me.'

She created safety amid the ruins. The other day I heard the old 5th Dimension song 'Up, Up and Away' on the radio and the hopeful happiness of my childhood rushed back. There's Mum grilling chops in the tiny kitchen of our rented flat, me wrapped in a vast bath towel in front of the gas fire, music playing on the radiogram. She let me eat dinner watching television with my plate perched on the wide arm of the sofa. If I woke in the dark, I found my way to her double bed; for months I didn't pretend to sleep anywhere else. I felt no envy of my friends with two parents, siblings and a big house. I had Mum all to myself.

At first she told me Dad was away working, which was often true, but postponed the whole truth. Mostly she knew just when to segue from fantasy to fact. For years she wrote Christmas cards *To Susie, from Santa* in an old man's shaky hand, but she came clean as soon as she saw realisation on my face. When I asked about babies while we were tidying the linen press, she gave me the details straight and then took me to the library.

But the Dad story was harder. I was six when she came in from the letterbox opening a cream envelope and stopped for a moment to read the letter before running up the hall to her bedroom. I found her flung across the bed and sobbing like a child, the sheet of paper hanging from her fingers. I clung to her legs and cried too.

Finally she said, 'Daddy isn't coming home.'

There were visits from Dad, tense conversations about money, and for me holidays with his new family and outings to climb trees, fly kites and catch fish. I was always glad to go home but, caught in a state of the emotional bends, I didn't show it enough. Mum swallowed her excitement and hid her hurt from her formal, cool-eyed daughter. We were so different, so often unknown to each other, and yet I can't imagine a more perfect mother.

'Image of her mother,' she said reflexively after she or anyone else paid me a compliment.

Mum was brave: she killed moths and spiders and fought off men who thought a divorced woman was easy prey. She was daring: she learned to drive, bought a Mini Minor and became famous for her tight U-turns and illegal parking. She was patient: not a harsh word, even when I vomited in the front seat of the Mini or peed in my sleep on her new sofa. She was modern: she worked hard, built a career and bought us a house. She was beautiful: her blonde curls turned white 'overnight' after her divorce but her blue-grey eyes shone, she was full and fresh and stylish even when her cheque account was in the red. She was vivacious: although she dreaded parties she laughed and danced and was often there until the end; strangers befriended her and men desired her. She was late: I was usually the last kid to be picked up from school and always seemed to be waiting. She was a generous spirit, open-minded, moral and wise. For a long, long time I believed she could solve any problem.

My life without her was unimaginable and I began imagining it from the first time I reached for her hand in a crowd and found a stranger attached. As an adolescent at home when she was late, I stared out the window and fought panic until I believed the night must end with a call from the police. She always turned up, oblivious and apologetic, just as I had begun to make hysterical calls to anyone who might track her down or take in her orphaned daughter.

We were like two teenagers when the seventies came. Mum was a friend to my friends, a role model of independence. We shared meals, diets and Woody Allen movies. She cheered my successes at school and I pushed her into acting classes. Our little house was alive with energy and laughter and Irish setters. But sex got in the way. Men and boys arrived and when things became serious we took turns to be jealous and protective.

The day I was cramming Latin for an important exam, Mum announced she was going out to lunch with the man who had transformed her from a mother into a lustful woman.

I responded to her threat of abandonment with a tantrum and, to my outrage, was delivered to my aunt's house to study while Mum went to lunch. Another year, Mum was planning to join my boyfriend and me for a distant picnic with friends. When it was time to set out she was drying her hair and putting on her makeup. We waited; we were late. 'We're going, Mum,' I said finally and as we headed for the door her enraged cry—'You bitch!'—hit the back of my head.

I was there, though, kneeling by her bed and stroking her hair, on the night of despair after her lover had strayed.

I left her too, of course, moving half a block down the street with my boyfriend and dogs, and then to other suburbs and other countries, jobs and marriages. Mum didn't complain—she paid my rent for the first year—but I felt a tug of guilt that she was the one at home alone.

'I don't think I'll ever marry again,' she said eventually and I agreed. She didn't really trust men—hers or mine—and who could blame her? There were offers, none of them irresistible, and by then she had found strength and comfort in solitude.

The second time she went to hospital, she had broken her elbows. Going to visit friends, she made her way in the dark and did not see the cracked concrete that rose up and tripped her. She hit the ground hands first. Her friend found her there and made one of those calls I'd always dreaded: 'Shirl's had an accident.' I was home for a visit from New York and rushed to the hospital.

Mum was pale with pain and the X-rays showed complicated fractures that would require surgery. Both arms in slings, she settled in as if at a health spa, in no rush to leave her pleasant room overlooking the garden, and the attention of the nurses. I was relieved to see her growing stronger in body and spirit. But what about the surgery? 'Oh, I don't think that will be necessary,' she said. She entertained the orthopaedic surgeon but politely resisted any pressure to schedule an operation. When I had to return to work in New York the hospital staff were gently trying to eject her.

There was no surgery. A final set of X-rays showed no sign of fracture. The surgeon was pleased but mystified: bones didn't mend so quickly. Mum explained lightly that she had been treated by a Christian Science practitioner and she was not at all surprised by the result.

Ah, here was the fulcrum on which her life turned. Whatever emptiness Mum felt, she filled it with her belief— her *knowledge*—that we are created by God's infinite love and our real existence is not material but spiritual. Her mother had learned about Christian Science in its heyday and the family adopted the teachings of its American founder, Mary Baker Eddy, who had healed herself and many others of physical and mental ills through prayer.

Mum was only in her twenties when first her mother and then her father died. Rather than losing her faith, she said Christian Science helped her to rise above her grief. She was private about her religion and never stern or dogmatic. For me it was natural to go to Sunday school, to learn lines I can still recite from Mrs Eddy's textbook *Science and Health*, and to turn to a practitioner for spiritual treatment, which dispelled fear and directed attention away from physical conditions to acknowledge God's power. We went to the dentist, I had vaccinations at school and a doctor came to our home when I had measles or Mum had hepatitis. But I don't remember going to a doctor's surgery until I was a teenager wanting a prescription for the Pill.

By the time I was an earthbound journalist, I had drifted from the church but I still found a meditative calm in its prayers. I respected Mum's beliefs and was glad for the certainty they brought her. I didn't question her testimonies of healing for which there was no other explanation. Sometimes, in a crisis, I asked for her help and her clear thinking always guided me to some kind of solution.

'Seventy is different,' she told me soon after her birthday celebration, when I gave her a diamond ring that she would only ever remove to polish and show me its sparkle. ('My Susie gave it to me,' she told admirers, flashing its modest constellation.) She was still a 'young' mother and I was surprised that she would make any concession to age. But she felt deeply tired and finally she gave up work.

'I don't know how people live to a hundred,' she said. 'The thought is exhausting.'

Living back in Sydney with my husband, I saw Mum when I could and talked to her on the phone, but she quietly craved a return to our old partnership.

'I thought you'd want to see more of me,' she said.

'I got used to living without you,' I tried to explain.

When I wrote my first book about a young man with a brain tumour, I didn't mean it as an insult to Mum. At first I was attracted to the story because the pianist seemed to have overcome his illness through a combination of a neurosurgeon's courageous work and his own spiritual strength. I thought it might prove something. To my surprise I became fascinated by the operating theatre and hospital ward, places of mystery and fear, and when his cancer returned I was plunged into a medical story with a sad ending. After the pianist died I sat by his bed, holding his hand, and wondered at the emptiness of his boyish body. I had only proved to myself that neither God nor doctors gave a guarantee.

My reliably proud mother, who clipped every newspaper story I wrote, came to the book launch and kept a copy on her coffee table to show visitors. But after reading the first few pages she laid the book aside and that was that. If I was disappointed, I also understood: while I needed to know how bodies functioned and failed, Mum did not.

As she approached eighty she moved into an apartment, sold her car and became dependent on others to take her places. But she was slower and later than ever, and our outings exhausted us all. Besides, she was more and more content to stay at home. 'I'm never lonely and never bored,' she declared.

We settled into a routine. On Saturdays I rang for her shopping list and delivered the week's supplies. 'Suse!' she said as I came through the door, her eyebrows raised as if my arrival were the happiest surprise she could imagine. Love and anxiety filled my chest. When I bent to hug my shrinking mother I felt like an adult towering over a vulnerable child.

We sat down for a cup of tea and talked about this and that. They were irreplaceable times and I tried to slow down and be patient. She only hinted at her problems. I knew she spoke regularly to a Christian Science practitioner and had visits from a Christian Science nurse, who changed a bandage on her leg and read with her. I could see she was in some pain and had a vague idea of what her ailments might be. Years ago she'd seen a doctor with no result and told me she intended to rely solely on Christian Science. Questions were batted away. 'How are you?' led nowhere. 'Just love me,' she said. When there was an opening she told me, 'I'm learning so much about man's relationship with God. I'm growing all the time and it's so exhilarating.'

At times—especially when Mum was unaware of my gaze—I had the strange sensation that I could see through her, as if her physical presence were diminishing and she hardly impressed herself on the air. Neither of us admitted that she had begun her gradual departure. I still believed in her extraordinary mother-power to fix things, or perhaps I was just in denial. I didn't want her to be old.

If I allowed myself to imagine her death I pictured her going to sleep and not waking up. Whenever she did not answer the phone, my childhood panic hit and I braced myself. My mind shied away from whatever came next and yet the fear sat low in my stomach. I could not see myself nursing her at the end and even said once, 'Mum, I don't think I'd be a very good carer.' Naturally she hated the thought of nursing homes and I wondered if her stoicism was partly a defence against being 'put' in one. I had no intention of doing so but I didn't know what the alternative would be if things got worse. Blindly I hoped we could continue as we were.

'I'm trying not to be a nuisance,' she said.

～

The year I took long-service leave I planned to travel, work on a novel and recuperate from thirty years' full-time journalism. I also wanted to spend better time with Mum. My aunt and cousin helped her even more than usual while I went to France for my first month of freedom. The cleaner and the nurse were regular visitors. My husband took hot cross buns for Easter, ice-cream and delphiniums for Mother's Day, and carried out the garbage. No one reported any dramas.

By late June I was ready to be more attentive: I would write in the mornings and spend afternoons with Mum. But suddenly she was worse. Weak and pale, she began sleeping for long stretches, sometimes more than twenty-four hours. The nurse was there most days, tending to the wound on her leg and helping her bathe and move with a walking frame. When she left I cooked and ate with Mum, half-watching television and talking. If I could feed her, I thought, I could keep her alive.

'Mum, do you want some medical help?' I asked, not for the first time. Usually she just said no. This time she added, without looking at me, 'It's too late anyway.' Then there was silence.

We were both trying so hard to cope in our different ways. Her secrecy, which was intended to protect me and avoid giving reality to sickness, simply multiplied my unnamed fears. Christian Science seemed to be letting us both down and yet I was not allowed to say so. I felt powerless or, worse, passive but if a doctor came, what would happen? She would become another medicated, grey figure in a hospital bed. Mum's wishes were clear and my frustrating duty was to follow them. I just wished I knew how to do it well.

I cried at home but only once in front of her and she shook her head and said, 'Don't.' Another time she said, 'The thing I worry about most is not being here for you when you go through this.' Tongue-tied at her selflessness, I could only squeeze out, 'No, you mustn't.'

Our days found a new pattern. Mum remained cheerful and uncomplaining. She sat in her nightie on the sofa, surrounded by papers, books and the diary that kept her days in order. I reached her by leaning down to kiss her head. She was grateful for every tiny thing I did and noted in her diary the details of our time together: *Susie came at 4 pm, brought coffee, made tea, chicken soup, etc. and made chicken and veg for dinner. We watched* First Tuesday Book Club *where they talked about* Cold Comfort Farm *by Stella Gibbons. Dear sweet Susie!*

This wasn't how I'd planned to spend my long-service leave but Mum's timing seemed almost deliberate. Between visits I tried to pretend my life was normal. I wrote distractedly, helped my father to move, even went away for a working weekend. In early August my husband and I took a stroll on a cold Saturday afternoon and peeped in Mum's window. She beckoned us in for a cup of tea. He hadn't seen her for weeks and she half joked that he wasn't welcome (no one was). He remembers her laughter following him out the door.

The following Saturday I had an all-day writing class. I dropped in early to leave breakfast beside Mum's bed, and during the day the nurse came and my aunt and cousin visited with homemade soup and pies. In the evening Mum was in her usual spot on the sofa but she seemed distant and confused. She asked to look at an artwork she had bought not long ago and pointed out dozens of non-existent dogs hidden in the abstracted scene. She seemed to be hallucinating.

'You're looking at me with real love,' she said, turning to focus her eyes on mine.

'You mean unlike all the other times?' I bantered back.

I heard myself and wondered why I couldn't stop the defensive cracks and just say, 'Yes, I love you so much. I love you more than I have ever told you. I love you enough to fill all the other gaps and wounds and make you whole.'

She was shivering so I turned up the heater. When I was about to leave she asked me to go out for takeaway Chinese and by the time I'd brought back the honeyed chicken and broccoli I was late for dinner with friends.

'Can't you stay for five more minutes?' she asked as she picked at her plate.

'No, Mum, I've got to go. I'm trying to do the right thing by everyone.'

What was I thinking? To be honest I was tired and spooked and wanted to get away. But at our friends' place I cried and wondered why I was there. Next morning a paralysing gloom fell over me. I knew I should be with Mum but I lay in bed and convinced myself she would contact me when she woke, as she often did. In the evening my cousin called to say she was there cooking dinner. Do you want me to come? I asked half-heartedly. She insisted I take a break and stayed deep into the night.

I was woken early on Monday by a call from the nurse, who had heard from the practitioner. Mum needed help. I hurried there, followed soon by the nurse. Mum was in bed and coherent but her breathing was fast and shallow. We supported her to the bathroom and brought water, tea and food she didn't want. It's hard to believe but I had been planning another short trip that week to speak at a writers' festival. With the nurse's agreement I went home and cancelled my arrangements and returned with a bunch of jonquils that I put in an orange vase beside Mum's bed. They looked like a child's drawing of spring flowers and made her smile.

As the day went on Mum chatted intermittently but she was restless and feverish. I told her to try to breathe more deeply and stroked her brow with a cool cloth. She dozed and woke. I rang the practitioner many times and held the phone to Mum's ear; she closed her eyes to take in the soothing words. The nurse came and went and when she left for the night I stayed by the bed without a plan.

'I'm not leaving, Mum,' I said. She looked relieved. I still did not know what dying looked like and it didn't occur to me that I should bring the family to her bedside. Perhaps unconsciously I felt we had to do this, whatever it was, together. One last time I offered to call a doctor or an ambulance and for a fearful moment wondered if I should call anyway—more for me than for Mum. Then I tried to apply myself to being there. I was intent on not falling apart and Mum's courage helped me but we were just being ourselves, mother and daughter. She asked me to call the practitioner and when there was no answer for a while Mum looked anxious.

'Even if we can't get her, you know the truth, Mum. You don't need her. I'm here, God's here, we're all here.' Her eyes were shut but her lips turned up in a half-smile.

'I've given my whole life to this,' she said. I assumed she meant Christian Science and perhaps preparation for her ultimate test.

'It suited your . . .'

'. . . psyche?' she said with a puff of laughter. She'd never talked much about psychology but maybe she was right.

'No . . . your view of life,' I said, hearing my absurd dryness.

I thought it might be a comfort for both of us if I lay on the bed and cradled Mum. But each time I tried to curl into her the phone rang and I leapt up, rocking the mattress. Even sitting beside her seemed an intrusion so I stood. She had windmilled herself sideways across the mattress and she looked tiny and fragile. But the hand pressed to her forehead was smooth and manicured—the hand that had always held mine, much too youthful for this.

I should have said I loved her but it came out differently. I wanted her to know she had succeeded at her life's work. I made sure to use the present tense.

'Mum, I couldn't have a more loving mother.'

'No,' she said, 'I don't think you could.' Her certainty almost made me laugh.

I don't know where she was drifting between our snatches of conversation, but the last I heard from her was 'Mum . . . Mum.' She might have been echoing the word she always loved hearing from me. I've since read that dying people sometimes call for their parents and Mum always said I reminded her of her mother, so perhaps at that moment we blurred. I hope she felt our love.

Some time after midnight, when Mum relaxed into sleep, I decided I should rest. Who knew how long this would continue?

Well, I didn't. I slept jammed into the two-seater sofa that I had peed on as a child. Mum's coughing woke me and I went into her bedroom where, by the half-light, I wiped her lips and stroked her back until she subsided again. On her digital clock I saw it was just after three and I tiptoed back to the sofa. When I woke again around five, I knew.

Mum was lying as I'd last seen her but there was an extra stillness to her. Her back was warm under my hand but didn't move; or did it? When I was sure, I went out and sat in the dark silence. I didn't cry, I didn't pray, I barely thought. I suppose I was beginning my slow acceptance. As dawn came through the blinds I was still sitting and it was time to do something. I rang the nurse, the practitioner, my aunt, my husband and, a few beats later, my father.

'She's gone,' I said. For a moment no one knew what I meant, and then they were stunned and began to hurry over.

I had to make another call, the nurse told me. Because Mum had died at home and had not seen a doctor in the past three months, the police had to be informed. This was the first I'd heard of that. Two young constables turned up at the scene of the possible crime, just as they had when I reported a burglary. They were polite but they had to examine Mum and interview me about the circumstances of her death. My skin prickled with automatic guilt. Two detectives in dark suits crowded into the living room to ask more questions and take photographs. One of them said he'd recently lost his grandmother and understood how I felt.

All the same, Mum would have to go to Glebe Coroner's Court, better known as the morgue. As a young journalist

I had covered inquests there and had glimpsed the nightmarish sight of a refrigerated storeroom lined with shelves of naked, fire-damaged bodies. It was unbelievable that Mum's carefully guarded, private withdrawal from the world should end in such indignity. I was outraged but useless. The police said we should remove her jewellery before she was taken away, and my husband stepped up to a task I couldn't do. He came out of the bedroom with the diamond ring I'd given her twelve years earlier and placed it on the table. I couldn't look at her again. I didn't say goodbye. And then, for a second time, she was gone.

On Mum's list of *Important Memories* the first note says: *Morning after Mummy died. The sun came up. Birds began to sing. The world went on as though nothing happened. Incredible!*

Nothing changes, and everything. In the days and weeks that followed, I went about the many things that had to be done, making the phone calls, arranging the funeral, giving the eulogy, applying successfully to stop the autopsy, holding myself together. A bubble of unreality separated me from the world and I wanted to shout through the invisible wall, 'My mother is dead!' Quietly I accosted acquaintances on the street, the girl who made my daily coffee, any stranger who casually asked how I was: 'My mother died yesterday.' 'My mother died last week.' No one seemed to register the importance of what I was saying. As the days slipped by I felt Mum disappearing into the past.

I cried in short storms, sometimes prompted by a kindness or a song or, just as often, by pushing my supermarket trolley past the bread and biscuits I no longer bought for Mum. Friends let me cry and talk. My husband held me tightly in bed. Grief entered my body as stabs of pain that gradually quietened to a low, humming ache. Mum had once said I seemed to take on her various complaints in sympathy and now mortality was my affliction. My future looked like an inconsequential moment. I took to reading every death notice in the newspaper out of respect for each individual loss and I noticed that all the Shirleys were dying. Soon, I thought, it would be all the Susans.

More than a year later I am still winded—sometimes several times a day—by the sudden realisation that *Mum is dead*. For an instant I think there must have been a mistake, until it sinks in once more that I will never see her again, that I cannot change anything that happened to her or between us. I miss her as much as I did on the first day, perhaps more. I feel like a table that has lost a leg; even with three good legs I wobble and teeter. She is my lost love.

And yet we find ways to cope. We create rituals and grow new parts. I did my best to follow Mum's six pages of notes, headed *Future Project*, on how to run her funeral. (*A thanksgiving service. Lovely flowers, lovely music, not too much serious religious stuff ... Whoever wants to speak can say nice things about me if they can think of anything or funny things if they want. Don't be too cruel, 'cause I've tried my best, like everyone. But, yes, be realistic.*) I slid her diamond ring onto my finger and wore it constantly for a year. I dedicated a tree to her in Sydney's Centennial Park, a favourite place planted with memories: a grand Moreton Bay fig almost as old as she was, with a broad shadow and deep hollows where I can sit in its embrace.

I took heart from a newspaper story that said seventy per cent of Australians wanted to die at home but in fact seventy per cent died in hospital, and that most doctors did not want to suffer the 'hell' they inflicted on their end-of-life patients. Perhaps I did not fail her, even if I could have done better.

At last I can see her—why did it take so long?—as more than my mother, as a woman and a daughter. Mum always spoke of her own mother as if she'd just left the room. Only now do I understand how devastating that early loss must have been for her and how it shaped her, how she idealised her mother and treasured the bond that I could treat more casually.

If ever I thought I would stop being my mother's daughter I know now that she'll always be in my head, praising me, curbing me, telling me I'm beautiful or should wear more eye makeup or lose weight or hold on to my job. A mother's power is inextinguishable.

Many months after Mum died, I found a letter that I had shoved among some old papers and forgotten. She'd written it in 1979 when I was twenty-one and living in London but had decided against sending it. Instead she handed it to me after I moved home from New York almost twenty years later, and although I read it then I did not absorb it as I have now. The two handwritten pages spell out her love for me (*my main reason for living*) and her hopes for my life based on her unwavering principles.

One day, she wrote, *if I should have to leave you to go on to another stage of experience, I hope you won't be sad, because I will be alright ... Love, love, love—be compassionate—to yourself as well as to others. Overflow with love—and be wise.*

This is my message to you—because I want you to enjoy life; it is a marvellous opportunity. Be courageous, fear nothing—for there is nothing to fear. I know this to be true. With love from your little mother.

IF YOU HAVE TEARS

GERARD WINDSOR

MY FATHER CRIED EASILY. I never saw him sob or weep at length, but on certain occasions he would be overcome, his voice would falter, and he would choke back tears. One or two at the most escaped him. Invariably these teary moments were occasioned by tributes—tributes he was paying. Even if he were receiving a tribute, any emotion he showed was because he was also hearing, at least as loudly, a tribute to some companion of his work. The constant object of his own tributes was his wife, my mother. When he made a birthday or anniversary speech, formally or informally, his children would wait for his emotional falter, but our slight embarrassment was balanced by an equal pleasure of confidence in his predictability. My mother appeared to accept it patiently. At least, patience seemed to be more on display than gratitude. I believe we all thought that was the right response. My father couldn't help himself, and we just put up with it and hoped that his biting his lip would do the trick and stem any flow.

I have only one memory of his tears being those of grief. As far as I know he had a fortunate life in that he lost to premature death only one of the people close to him. His parents lived to a good age, none of his six children died young, he predeceased all but one of his siblings, and that one was killed in 1942, before my time, and I never saw any subsequent grief or even anything like a commemoration of the anniversary. But when I was seven and my sister six, my parents' third child, a toddler, contracted encephalitis, and I remember my father crouching down and putting an arm around each of us and saying, 'We think little Johnny might die.' He was crying then.

My father died when he was seventy-two. For five years he had had cancer spreading through and from his bowel. He underwent surgery four times. His family had fair warning of his decline and inevitable death. When he was first diagnosed, it had been only six years since his own father's sudden death just before his ninety-first birthday. When I learned my father had cancer, part of the jolt I felt was from this irregular cramming up of the generations, this refusal to allow them their rightful twenty-five-year free breathing space. Had it not been for an accident, my grandfather might well have been still alive and active when his eldest son was given his terminal diagnosis. Having spent his day seeing patients, the old man had got up from his armchair to turn off his television for the night, but his movement must have been too abrupt and maybe he had a moment of dizziness, because he tripped over his radiator and fell and broke some ribs. Pneumonia set in and he was dead within days.

From about 1971 I had got into the habit of taking the train up from Sydney to Brisbane once or twice a year to stay with my grandfather. By this time he had been a widower for fifteen years and he lived in an old apartment on Wickham Terrace with his housekeeper, a widow herself and almost as elderly. He didn't go to bed till about midnight because he preferred the longueurs of the evening to their even more desolate form in the small hours of the morning, and he was delighted to have company. He and I talked a lot—about his homeland, Ireland, where I spent seven months in 1973, and about family—his parents, his only sibling, a girl who had died at eighteen, about his wife and their courtship and her protracted dementia, about his children and their spouses, about those of his grandchildren who had reached adulthood and so were definable individuals to him. On his part, so much of this ruminative talk was analytical and frank and even critical. But he shone the light too on himself, on those moments and decisions he still worried over—his refusal to return to Ireland to be with his lonely father, his possible harshness towards a son that caused the boy to run away and go mechanical rather than professional and then learn to fly and join the air force and so die in the North Sea.

My grandfather gave me the confident feeling of my being a desirable, equal companion. As a child I would never have predicted this. He was not interested in small children; he was tall and shortsighted and his voice and manner seemed gruff, partly because of his County Tyrone accent overlaid by his years studying and practising medicine in Scotland and England, and then in Queensland. But as I approached thirty I realised my grandfather found me someone whose conversation and activities were of lively interest to him. A rational expectation might have been that given the spottiness of my career to date my grandfather would have been censorious. I was a spoiled priest, and when I entered the Jesuit novitiate my father had warned me to be sure of my decision because 'if you leave . . . well, your grandfather could tell you what pathetic creatures those fellows turn out to be'. But my grandfather neither adverted to, nor even appeared to skirt, the issue, and gave no sign at all of regarding me as a pathetic individual. Then, even during the years I was visiting him, I enrolled in and subsequently dropped out of medicine. Outsiders might have expected him to be elated at the prospect of a third generation going into the profession and then commensurately disappointed at my failure, but I never felt nor heard any such reaction. If anything he seemed proud of me; he liked to take me around with him and introduce me to people. I went with him on a medical visit to the Carmelite nuns at Ormiston, and he introduced me through the grille and told the few nuns who could crowd to that peephole—and told them with almost boastful pride—that I had been commissioned to write the history of a school. Yet I myself hardly regarded this as a high point on a CV.

There was immense pleasure, for both of us I think, in this friendship. When I left for Sydney my grandfather got into the habit of giving me the train fare and a bit more, and he said to me, 'I almost hate you coming, because it's so hard when you go away.' He had tears in his eyes. From all the years of my childhood and youth I remember no other declaration of love as I remember this one.

So, when he was buried from St Stephen's Cathedral, the inhibitors were all down. The crowd, the music, all the great biblical and liturgical phrases intoxicating the air, I cried. Apart from the tears of childhood I don't remember ever having done so before. I hadn't cried three and half years previously when my maternal grandmother died, yet I know I loved her—a warm, intelligent, spirited woman. But I suppose she had never become a companion to me, not in the prime of her life, which is where my grandfather somehow still was, even at ninety.

I suspect that I went home from my grandfather's funeral with a sense of completeness and gratitude. Certainly not with any sense of disorienting loss. I have never suffered a death that has torn me apart, or left me stunned and functionless. I have never lost a child or a wife or a sibling. Yet I live surrounded by family and friends who have lost childen to cot deaths and drug overdoses and car accidents and medical mishaps, and it is beyond me how they cope and can have continuing interests, even passions, and can laugh. There is a vast emotional terrain there that they have covered, and I haven't so much as put a foot on it, and their human experience reminds me just how slight and superficial mine is. Without losses such as theirs I can never quite know what grief is. And of course I'll do anything to avoid paying the price for that extension of my understanding and sympathies. If I'm allowed to go on unscathed in this way, I'll always be backward. Whatever empathy I might develop, it would be arrogant and presumptuous to think I had reached up to the understanding of anybody who had suffered the extremes of grief.

For all the deaths I've witnessed, for all the countless funerals I've attended, I've been somehow shielded. Or I've been introduced painlessly. My first death in the family, as it were, occurred when I had just turned eighteen. I was one of twenty-three new Jesuit novices, and had been so for only a week, when we all walked out one hot February day into the Yarra country and went swimming, and one of our number, Michael Liston, drowned. I had barely met him, and I don't remember being knocked down by shock or by any intimation of my own mortality. Only later, decades later, did I begin to sense the horror for Michael's still-young parents, and the guilt that must have lodged permanently in the senior novice looking after Michael on that day and in the priest, the novice master, into whose care he'd been entrusted, both of them good, sensitive human beings. But I fear that at the time, and for an unconscionable time afterwards, Michael Liston's death was, for me, a story, a dramatic, jaw-dropping story of chaos in the yawningly placid routine of a novice's life.

Within a year I was present at my first deathbeds. Of men I had no connection with—except that I was caring for them, in an amateurish professional way. I was still an eighteen-year-old Jesuit novice, doing a stint as a nurse's aide, at Caritas Christi Hospice for the Dying in Kew. There was Mr Portelli, a blind old man in a cot who sucked Kool Mints and shared them with us; a Polish man in his early thirties, a husband and father, sweating through the last fevers of his brain tumour; Daniel Mannix, ninety-nine and suddenly collapsed, having to be lifted into bed still in his cassock. I was moved, and I was stilled, by these encounters, but I wasn't pained by them.

For a man not actually in the medical or pastoral professions I've had some strange deathbed experiences. About 1987 I had to visit the composer Malcolm Williamson, home in Sydney on an extended visit and resident in a swanky apartment in Elizabeth

Bay. Williamson and I were not friends—largely because his life partner, Simon Campion, was one of my oldest friends. What with some drink taken and the underlying ill will, the visit ended badly; Williamson followed me out to the lift and as I stepped into my getaway vehicle his curse rang through the lift well: 'God damn you and all your fucking family for all eternity.' Our intercourse ceased there. Sixteen years later, in 2003, I was in London, and Williamson had had a stroke and was in hospital in Cambridge, and Simon asked me to visit him. 'Just chat to him,' he said. So I went up to Cambridge. Williamson lay propped up in bed and his eyes drilled into me with a fierce, fixed stare. But he had lost all power of speech. Not even a movement of the lips. Now where were we? I asked. But not aloud. I chatted—the appetising appearance of the food, the outlook of the hospital, the Howard government, Simon's virtues ... To abuse the adjective as it is commonly abused, the episode was painful.

Real pain is a different matter. How much of that have I felt? I've never been confronted by a sudden or accidental death. Not of any intimate. I go on towards my own end, and companions falter and fade, but no one, as it happens, has just dropped off precipitately. Instead, cancer strikes all around me. Between my drafting and finishing this essay, Rosie Fitzgibbon, in her early sixties, my long-standing editor and friend, succumbed to a brain tumour. Peter Alexander, biographer and friend for over thirty years, hopes the cancer in his spine will let him see out the year. A sister-in-law who never smoked fights the primary in her lung.

Spontaneously I rally round. I see these friends more than I would if they were healthy. And I suspect that this might be more for my own sake than theirs, that I know now that their company, their friendship, which I have so long taken for granted, will not be endlessly available to me, and greedily I snatch at it as it moves towards the dark. Is this some form of anticipatory grief? The sense of imminent loss shadows in, giving me the time to catch up and repair and finalise that which the consummated loss will not allow me. What do I do on these last-chance occasions? Check the stories that I've forgotten or never been quite sure of; relive the days we've had together; tell them what they've meant to me (and bring it home to myself); ask, lamely enough, if there's anything I can do; repeat, even more lamely, that I'm thinking of them, praying for them.

Is this grief? The ache of pain is hardly its dominant feature. But there is the panic of deprivation, the sense that the dimensions of my life are being lopped and constricted. And the stark realisation that for these friends their biographies are now complete, that they've had the sum total of the experiences that define their lives. Nothing more to look forward to, to explore, to be converted by. Terminus.

As ever the appalled sympathy rebounds, now tense and frozen, and pummels me. Waste not! Repair! Be ready!

Some events I can prepare for. But it would be rash to anticipate my reaction to them. My mother is ninety-four and bedridden and with short-term memory loss. Yet she is capable of such long, even relentless, conversation, particularly in the interrogative form, that I sense a continuing richness of mental life, and I worry that through ennui and laziness I don't tap into it more, for both our sakes. My mother remains maternal in two distinct ways. She thanks me for ringing or coming to see her or preparing her a meal, and she exhorts me, as she does all her sons, to go to her purse for any trip to the shops and to get home before it's dark and to borrow her umbrella and to get to bed early. Just as she also admonishes me for being unshaven or not wearing a tie or missing mass or travelling just for pleasure. She is perceptive and gracious and sharp, and there has been no passage from our being parent and son into being easy companions. My dispassionate judgment is that I am not my mother's favourite child—and I feel no resentment at that—but I think that some of my brothers may have passed over into more obvious friendship with her. What will all this mean when she dies? To varying degrees the lives of her five sons centre around attendance on her, and her absence will inevitably realign all the plates. But grief? I can't say.

Pathetically perhaps I fall back on tears. I get teary easily, although I must belong to the last generation where the principle reigned that men don't cry. What do the tears mean? Being prone to tears is a physiological trait, and says little about depth of feeling. After all, any competent actor can turn on tears. All the same, some tears are not just crocodilian or staged. My father's certainly weren't. But I don't think his tears were a response to loss or a manifestation of grief. As a cardiac surgeon he had patients die while in his care. He would be abstracted and depressed when this happened, and my mother would tell us that he had lost a patient, and very briefly the family mood might be a little more sombre. But there were never tears. Nor did I see tears for any more private or familial loss.

Tears were a tribute. My mother, as I said, elicited them most, above all for her supportiveness. But they appeared on other occasions too. In August 1945, serving with the 14th Australian General Hospital, my father had been instructed to locate the Australian Army nurses who were prisoners of the Japanese. We knew of this because he was mentioned a couple of times in Betty Jeffrey's memoir, *White Coolies*. But in the years of his final illness, when he began to write memoirs of his own, we prodded him on this coda to his war. He had located the nurses and arranged for Matron Sage, their matron-in-chief, to fly to Lahat in Sumatra where they were being held. There were two emotional danger points in this story. One was my father ensuring that he stood back and that Matron Sage was the first off the plane and the first to greet the women. The second was Matron Sage asking, 'Where are the rest of you?' and the women answering, 'This is all of us, Matron.' I was about to say that my father faltered and had to bite his lip at these points. But now I hesitate to do so. The trouble is that when I tell this story myself I falter at these points and the tears come to my eyes. To muddy the memory still further, I wrote my own version of the story but in the context of an encounter between my father and myself. And I attribute an imminence of tears to both of us, but now I don't think that was true of my father. I myself teared up, but although that was mostly because of the poignant drama of the scene, it was also because I was moved by and admired my father's sensitivity.

I always admired my father. Yet when he died I don't remember that I shed tears. What did this mean? The impediment, I think, was that my father and I never became companions. I never felt completely at ease with him. In part this was because I felt he was disappointed in me and hence disapproved of me. I wouldn't blame him for this. Had I been my own father, I think I would have been disappointed and disapproving—and irritated and occasionally censorious as well. The objective facts were that I had shown a lot of promise at school, then had embraced two careers and walked away from them both, had written a commissioned book which had been suppressed, had done a bit of this and a bit of that but not very much, had been sexually irregular . . . My father never exploded at any of this, and the guarded reticence between us, the unwillingness to approach inflammable topics, was arguably all my doing. But unease was the result.

Near the end of his life I think that my father came to accept that if I were to be doing anything professionally it was to be writing. Before he died I had published two books of stories, and the second of these contained my version of his story about the rescue of the POW nurses. I was told by other people that sometimes, in front of some of his many visitors, he waved this book and said, 'Have you read this story in here?'

My father was a particularly fine human being. He was an involved, often playful father, a devout keeper of the flame for his wife, a hard-working and innovative surgeon who had no motivation other than to help the sick, a writer of family doggerel, a student of Mandarin, a pioneer from the 1960s of medical ties between China and Australia, a one-time rugby centre for New South Wales, a possessor of the gentlest and most appealing bedside manner who gave the most soothing sponges and least painful of injections. He was blessed in that he knew what his life was for, and never seemed to waver in his private or professional vocation. I admired my father enormously, and I believe all his children did.

Yet he and I never became mates, pals, friends. I think it must also have had something to do with our separation from one another in the first five years of my life. When my father came to write his memoirs, he recorded how he had obtained his Master of Surgery degree early in 1944. He was on active service in New Guinea, but the front had receded and things were quiet, and his CO, knowing the University of Sydney was about to hold its Master of Surgery exam, told him to hitch a ride on an aircraft coming south. He did so, only to miss the exam by a day. But the authorities, thinking it not fair to spurn a man serving his country, set an extra exam just for him. This was late March 1944 and he records that he passed and returned to the war. What he doesn't mention, quite understandably, is that I, his first child, was born in late December 1944.

He wasn't demobbed until August 1946. Then in 1947 he sailed to Britain for postgraduate work. He wanted my mother, with two children by this time, to accompany him, but she refused, believing that only the magnet of his family in Australia would ensure he returned here, which he finally did in October 1949. So he was largely absent for the first five years of my life—and for the first four of my sister's, who probably had the most problematic relationship with him. Both she and I wrote about our father. In my account of his story of the nurses I sum up these separated years as: *my father had chosen his ground. I wasn't on it then, or ever.* Twenty-seven years later I wonder that I published this story in my father's lifetime, and that I gave it to him to read. Not because I think it was critical of him, but because it dissected the inadequacies of our relationship, or at least my uncertainties, and that could only have been unsettling for a dying man.

Scripta manent, however. For some time I'd been aware that an entry on my father for the *Australian Dictionary of Biography* was being prepared by my old friend John Carmody, a doctor, historian of medicine and fellow old boy, with my father, of Gregory Terrace. A mutual friend told me he'd seen a draft of the entry, and thought it very good. He added neutrally that it made the point that my father was emotionally withheld, and that his family had suffered from his commitment to surgery. I believed this was quite inaccurate, that far from being emotionally withheld my father had been an old softie, and that he had been a fine husband and an inspiring, attentive and devoted father. The trouble, I thought, was the paucity of the witnesses called. The pool of potential testifiers had not been fished. As if there were only two people who could witness to my father's familial temperament—the two who had published on the subject—my sister and myself. It recalled to my mind a howler in a book on the murdered cardiac surgeon Victor Chang by the late Dick Hall, who wrote that Harry Windsor had to an extent adopted Chang as his protégé as a substitute for his own son, who had left home and committed himself to a life as a Jesuit. An interesting enough theory—as long as you haven't made yourself aware that Harry Windsor had in fact five sons.

My lack of ease with my father had not, I think, been shared by my younger brothers. My father was present throughout their childhood and youth, he went on camping trips and fishing holidays with them, he studied and discussed their school texts with them—he came close to knowing every word of *White Fang*, *All Quiet on the Western Front* and *In Cold Blood*. And there was a host of other binders: they were all better at sport than I was, one of them did medicine (and his father did it with him, he said), their personalities were less precious than mine, more committed to lives of unostentatious service. They were on my father's ground, and he on theirs.

So I wrote to John Carmody and told him all this. I had been stung that his version of my father was to become the official, permanent one, given the stamp of definitiveness by its appearance in the *ADB*. Of course I knew all about the writer having autonomy, but I believed that if I was objecting to the final portrait, it was because of the limited and tainted sources used. Which obviously implicated me myself. A short story is not a biographer's account of a man, and my awkwardness with my father was no ground for a universal rendition. Nevertheless I had written a version of him and a biographer would have been remiss not to have snapped it up.

It was a matter of justice. I didn't cry when my father died. There was no sense of a gaping, painful wound. I wasn't the least bit of an emotional mess. If that's moral, or at least emotional, retardation, I've got to wear it. Of course I can argue that I'd had five years to prepare and so there was no shock involved. But maybe, and more importantly, in the longer term grief was subsumed into this demand for justice, a tribute more palpably useful to the dead than grief.

Given the disconcerting wisdom that all men need, and wish for, the death of their fathers, what does that mean for our grief? We wouldn't be too likely to cry for the man we wanted dead.

But if we also loved him? As I think I did—I certainly admired and was grateful to him, enormously so. Surely we have to be left with a residue of guilt? A man condemned by the mere fact of being a father? At the very least we want justice for him. Or I did. If I had to get rid of him because he cramped my autonomy merely by being a concerned father, the father I recall is a man with nothing malign or injurious about him. I have a welter of affectionate memories of him—in an armchair, his reading to my sister and myself as tiny children; his unwillingness ever to administer more than a token tap of the wooden spoon on the hand when his children had to be punished; in Centennial Park, his reading aloud to me, as we walked together, the opening pages of *A Tale of Two Cities*; his ducking out from hospital one day in 1954 and returning from Angus & Robertson with half a dozen Dickens, and tearing off and binning the dustwrappers as was his wont, and writing and pasting into *Oliver Twist* a card addressed to the children he then had *in the hope that these may remain their lifelong friends*.

He was his father's son; the old man once said to me, 'I could salivate over a sentence of Dickens.' And maybe, all three of us, cry over one too.

FRED AND JOAN AT THE FORUM DES IMAGES

LINDA NEIL

About three weeks before my mother Joan died in June 2010, my brother Stephen, who had been her full-time carer for several years, called all her children living in various parts of Australia. He let each of us know that the muscles in Mum's throat that controlled her swallowing were no longer working properly and that we should come to say our goodbyes as soon as we could. He had known for a long time that once she could no longer take in food through her mouth, her death was imminent. After witnessing for a decade Mum's slow decline through Parkinson's disease, we had all agreed that, after Stephen's care had extended her life beyond what would have been possible in an institution, we would not put Mum on machines or life support in order to prolong her life.

She was moved into palliative care after a touching few days when Stephen, whose relationship with Joan was protective, practical and tender, fretted over her not being able to die at home in the house she had shared with him. Both my father and Joan's mother had died at home with reminders of their lives around them and it seemed fitting after Mum's long illness that she would have that good fortune as well. An acceptable compromise was reached when Stephen realised that to Mum home was not the house near the sea that they shared; it was, rather, his physical presence. He felt easier when he drew up the timetable of our visits to the hospital and decided to spend the nights in a small camp bed in her room. So while Mum may not have been able to die at the house she had lived in, she was going to die very close to home.

In many ways it was a luxury to have the time to gather together to observe and honour the daily process of dying in such an intimate and detailed way. As Mary, one of the Irish nurses at the hospice, told us: 'It's a strange and precious process that you are lucky to witness.'

That's not to say that deep emotion didn't regularly and intermittently well up: the moments when you could see her struggling for breath; the exhausted, sometimes clashing emotions of her children, and the peace that Stephen brought to us when he arrived for his evening shift; the tender understanding of Mum's grandchildren, who communicated by their uncharacteristic stillness in the room that they were not baffled by what was taking place. They had been born into and grown up through Joan's illness; they had never known her any other way.

A strange glow settled around her at times; I may have been imagining it, but Mary agreed with my description when I shared my impressions with her.

'I always think it looks like twilight,' she confided in her comforting Irish lilt. 'And I try to discourage families and loved ones from switching on the fluorescents. We should make the atmosphere as soft as possible. But some people feel uncomfortable in half-light; they need starker things to help them believe that the living will prevail over the dead. They think if they give death reverence it might swallow them up too.'

The light can be explained rationally, but even the doctor who came every evening to check on Mum's progress, if moving towards death can be called progress, seemed to recognise that some things that were happening were not strictly scientific. Perhaps he would have called it reverence as well, not in a religious sense, but in its secular reference to awe and perhaps amazement at the ongoing processes of life and death as sometimes inexplicable occurrences.

His favourite sayings reflected his reassuring pragmatism —'It's to be expected . . . mmm . . . perfectly normal'—whether he was talking about physical or emotional phenomena, though he did once add: 'She is lucky you are here. But then, you are lucky too.'

During her final days, Mum's breath came in short, sudden gasps. For a woman who'd taught so many would-be singers to breathe it seemed fitting that life in the end would be signified or not by breath: its presence, the sometimes painful release of it, its final absence. During the last days, as the struggle became more audible, I thought sometimes of Dylan Thomas's poem to his father: *Do not go gentle into that good night / Rage, rage against the dying of the light*. I didn't want Mum or anyone else to rage; the time for that had passed. And it was moving to see how the strange resonance in the room made us more, not less, gentle as she slipped further away. I wondered at the time whether there was a comparable poem that spoke of acquiescence to, rather than rage against, the dying of the light. I couldn't think of one. But as Mum often used to say, there is a time for everything. And I suspect, if she was still conscious of such things, that she would have known this was her time to leave us.

I recently recalled these last weeks of Mum's life in Paris where, in the space of twenty-four hours, I was touched by three of the things that touched her life: poetry, song and dance. In itself the confluence of these three art forms in the city that honours them on a daily basis wasn't remarkable. That all three seemed inextricably linked on that day to the memory of Mum and my still-present grief at her death might qualify in some contexts as significant. But this is Paris after all, the city of love and light in so many fantasies, but also, with its buildings and churches the colour of bone, its famous catacombs full of rotting skulls, and its history of convulsion and renewal, the city of the dead as well.

Some say the living mirror the dead in order to give them the comfort that life has some kind of continuity. Even before Mum died I was trying to continue her legacy as a singer and teacher, which I only fully appreciated during the period I was her carer, by becoming a writer and performer of songs myself. This new musical activity, which I developed in the early days of her illness with her help and guidance, found its form as a kind of alternative to what Mum's illness eventually meant: the loss of music, the loss of joy. As long as I could learn to sing and perform as Mum did, I rationalised to myself, her life would continue, as would mine. So I sang and composed as often as

I could. By doing so I learned how to use my breath, not just to endure and survive, but to articulate through the songs I created the connection, vitality and hope that Mum's disease seemed existentially to threaten.

Writing and singing words and melodies and sharing them with others became my defence against my own despair. Neurologically speaking, this musical activity was also, I discovered later, training my brain to rise up high into a kind of lightness, as my voice did as it sang a melody. Sharing the songs with others, something I eventually did through a series of what I called 'love song concerts', which were like tiny eulogies to my dying mother, meant also that this neurological alternative to the depression and anxiety that gripped her at the worst period of her Parkinson's experience could be transmitted to others. As for dancing, my lack of ability in that area is one of my regrets, although the violin, which Mum first arranged for me to study as a child, sometimes seemed during my years of improvising and performing on the instrument a kind of partner in a self-devised musical dance.

These things came back to me one Sunday in Paris at the end of an unseasonably cold spring in 2012. I was browsing the secondhand bookshelves outside Shakespeare and Company when I read these words by Rilke in an anthology of poetry about grief.

It's possible I am pushing through solid rock
in flintlike layers, as the ore lies, alone;
I am such a long way in I see no way through,
and no space: everything is close to my face,
and everything close to my face is stone.

I stayed with this poem for quite a while. The words made me think of Mum's passing, not because she knew Rilke's poetry—unless it was set to Schubert's music she generally preferred lighter verse—but because for several months after Mum died my face felt, and sometimes looked, like stone. It was shock, I suppose, cumulative and ongoing, that made me unable to smile or even cry. One counsellor I saw called it similar to post-traumatic stress.

My face like stone was perhaps another case of the living mirroring the dead. By the time she died, Parkinson's disease had slowly turned Mum's face and body rigid, and it had been impossible for her to smile or sing. Although I played the violin at her funeral, I didn't sing, nor could I for many months afterwards. The silence of stone also challenged, as grief sometimes does, all the hope and joy that my songs had brought to me and to others. Flints of that stone were still in my face the day I read Rilke's words. And I wondered that Sunday, as I had often during the nearly two years since Mum had died, if my face would ever move properly again.

I didn't buy the book, but left it for someone else to find, randomly, as I had. I began to walk back across the bridge, past the perfectly ordered stone of Notre Dame where tourists were already lining up with their cameras. I hadn't yet been inside the church, or inside any church since Mum's funeral. On most days I would turn right, walk through the square, straight past the cathedral and head back towards pont Saint-Louis, which would take me across the Seine to where I was living in a small writer's studio in the Marais. But that day I didn't turn. I suddenly realised the habits that I thought might keep me grounded in this sometimes overwhelming city were in the process of becoming set in stone as well. So for a change I kept walking in the direction of Bastille, and after a short while arrived at Starbucks, where sometimes I read Saturday's papers on a Sunday morning while sipping a tea latte made with soy milk.

There, I settled myself in one of my preferred window seats from where I could look out on the footpath and began to browse through the *International Herald Tribune*. On page three, I came across an obituary of the German baritone Dietrich Fischer-Dieskau, who had been one of Mum's favourite singers. He specialised in the Schubert Lieder, those perfect duets between singer and pianist that she loved so much. As I scanned the obituary, my eye settled on a couple of lines that made me think, suddenly aching, of how Mum, who honoured lyrics as much as melody, would advise her students to speak the words of a song out loud, like a poem addressed to an intimate friend.

In the manner of the great musical theater performers, the article read, *Mr. Fischer-Dieskau sang as if he were speaking . . . There was nothing quite like his voice, a rich, warm, textured baritone. He could dip into his low range and soar high, sounding mellifluous and lyrical.*

Starbucks on Rue de Rivoli wasn't exactly conducive to the outpouring of emotion, or the cracking of stone, but without any embarrassment at all I found myself weeping noisily as I read about the passing of this singer who, like my mother, was now a memory in the minds of those whose art and craft and lives he—they—had touched.

The welling up I experienced at Starbucks was abnormal only in its vocal intensity. Such things have happened frequently since Mum died, especially during the recent cold months in Paris, a seasonal aberration that seemed to align perfectly with my need to stay indoors quietly and fully experience what I won't hesitate to call deep sorrow.

Philosophy, religion and art all offer consolations to this sorrow, but grief also needs practical solutions. Sometimes you have to wait a long time for the solutions to arrive, just as in Paris this year the long extended winter has taken many of us in the city who have bent and shivered through the bleakest days way past what once might have been called our 'breaking point', the point beyond which we think we can't endure.

In Paris this year the spring has been so cold it feels as if winter hasn't thawed, and never will. It has been an ideal time in this city—one that Mum had a chance to visit the year before she first became ill, over ten years before she finally died—to grieve. And to discover that grief can have the quality of a long winter that seems as if it will never end: cold, dark, frequently wet, with a sense of interminability that after a while turns into acceptance. And a feeling that, like the cold, grief will never fully pass. 'Yes,' you think, looking out of a cafe window during the last week of official spring during which you have rarely seen the sunshine. 'This is the way things are now. This lack of light. This stone in my face.'

Later that day, as I was walking back from Place de la Bastille, where I had done my weekly fruit and vegetable shopping at the Sunday market, I passed a bus shelter that encased a large colour poster advertising *Paris vu par Hollywood*, a month-long season of Hollywood films set in Paris. The films were being shown at the Forum des Images, the cinema archives centre in Les Halles dedicated to preserving cinema from France and from many other parts of the world. The poster had an image of Audrey Hepburn from the film *Funny Face*. Wearing an exquisite red dress, she was standing like a model on a runway with her arms raised in a gesture that triumphantly called attention to her technicolour radiance. I stopped in front of the poster and recalled Mum talking excitedly about this film when I was a child as we sat down together to watch it on television one Sunday afternoon, much like this one, in Brisbane where I grew up.

'Oh yes, Audrey Hepburn is beautiful,' she told me. 'She is divine. But wait till you see Fred!'

I had no idea who or what Fred was. But I knew that in anticipation of him appearing with the divine Miss Hepburn, Mum had hurriedly taken off the apron she'd been wearing in the kitchen, smoothed her dress against her still lovely white legs, patted her blonde curls, and sat down beside me with a smiling sigh. Or a sighing smile. As the film began, she whispered excitedly, 'Ah, Fred Astaire! You know, they called him a cloud in top hat and tails.'

'A cloud in top hat and tails.' The image my mother gifted me with that day has stayed with me ever since. After months of my face hardened into stone by the memory of her suffering and death, I suddenly remembered the joy of watching *Funny Face* with her; and of first understanding that, in defiance of the bones in his body, a man, and possibly a woman, could work so hard and yet float so lightly and elegantly through the air that it seemed as if he had upended the order of things, and that weightlessness, grace and beauty could be like a revolution too.

I was so startled by the memory that I dropped my bag of fresh tomatoes and helplessly watched them scatter, as red as the red of Audrey's dress, all over the pavement. One of them, soft and bruised already, burst open as it rolled into the gutter. I looked around guiltily for witnesses, but, perhaps because of the cold, this part of Rue de Rivoli was momentarily deserted and I was alone with my broken bag and my memories.

I didn't quite understand the rush of emotion I suddenly felt watching the squished tomato coming to rest in the gutter. But as my breath shortened and my heartbeat became noticeably rapid I knew what I was feeling was a brief unfamiliar surge of elation. For the first time in many months, I had a clear idea of where I was headed. I turned and walked back down Rue de Rivoli towards Les Halles.

I knew that the Forum had a film on Sundays at four pm, but I didn't know what film was on that day. I did know, though, that if I walked fast I might just make the afternoon session; I would take my chances on what I would see when I got there. I knew that this was something Mum would have loved to do if she had been here with me: see a classic film on the big screen and experience it anew watching it with a Parisian audience. And although lately my body had felt as stiff and weighty as an old woman's, I moved more lightly than usual as I hurried down Rue de Rivoli towards the Forum des Images.

I arrived for the afternoon session late, out of breath, hair and face a mess, laden with plastic shopping bags full of ripening fruit and vegetables. The cashier looked at me disapprovingly. The film had already started.

'It always starts directly on time, no matter what,' he told me in French.

'*C'est bien pour moi*,' I assured him in my basic French. 'Do you know what it's called?' I then asked him in English.

'*L'Entreprenant Monsieur Petrov*,' he replied.

I didn't have a clue how that might translate, other than the entrapment of a Russian man called Mr Petrov. Possibly a Cold War spy movie, I thought, though it didn't sound like any classic I had heard of. But I didn't want to press the attendant for more detail. I bought my ticket, walked upstairs, expecting little but suddenly happy to be here, and headed into the dark.

As I felt my way up the aisle and my eyes grew accustomed to the gloomy cinema, the room was suddenly illuminated. I looked up at the screen and was almost blinded by the light of a scene in which Fred Astaire was tap dancing around what looked like a ship's engine room, accompanied by a makeshift band of African American musicians. The set was stark white art deco and Fred's feet moved at a blistering pace as he traversed the area, tapping, pirouetting, twirling, stomping, sometimes with his coat slung casually over his shoulder as if literally nothing would ever weigh him down.

I scanned the rows for an empty seat and saw that many of the audience were women who could have been my mother: neatly dressed ladies with sensible short permed hair styles— Mum's, though, was naturally curly—their faces luminous in the reflected glow of the screen. There were young people there too, dancers, I thought, or classic film buffs, and gentlemen, together or alone, all gathered in the dark like a congregation in a church waiting for light, for music, for meaning, for all the things that people expect at a funeral and which, frozen in sorrow, I hadn't been able to access at Mum's nearly two years before. I sat down near the aisle at the back and took my first seated breath. The effect of being in the cinema was visceral. My nerves were tingling, my heart aching, my face creaking, my chest heaving.

During the next hour or so I began to think there was nothing on earth like watching a film with a Parisian audience, who laugh at all the jokes, who sigh at the dancing, smile along with the songs, ooh and aah at the costumes, who seem to understand so deeply in ways I don't, but perhaps my mother did, the meaning, the longing, the dreaming of a film.

The film itself, called *Shall We Dance* in English, had a typically silly storyline: a Russian classical dancer falls in love and eventually, after devious plans backfiring and various misadventures, pairs up with an American showgirl. The metaphor of Fred and Ginger in the film perfectly aligned with the highbrow/lowbrow amalgamation that Mum always championed. The film, which I later discovered was scored especially for the screen by the Gershwins, featured some songs that I first heard my mother sing in our living room, like 'They Can't Take That Away From Me', and 'Let's Call the Whole Thing Off', with its memorable lyrics.

Watching the film on a full-sized screen, I noticed things I'd never been able to pick up on television or a DVD: that while Ginger seemed solid, grounded and a little weighty, even though she was a slim and delicate woman, Fred moved as if he had no normal sense of gravity. And also how much Ginger, dancing awkwardly on roller skates, looked like a saucier, earthier version of my mother when she was young. In fact, sometimes as I watched I imagined it was Mum up there on the screen lifted and guided by the man beside her—Fred and Joan, not Fred and Ginger—as if they were two silver ghosts dancing on air through a black-and-white sky.

Finally the last scene arrived. On a mirrored set, surrounded by multiple versions of Ginger who, dressed in black satin, danced across the stage like multiple versions of my dead mother, Fred, in his top hat and tails, sang the film's title song: 'Shall We Dance'. Listening to its upbeat rhythm, I had the thought, aching again, that Mum might have chosen this particular song for her own funeral, not just as a means for us to mourn her, or because she loved musical comedy as much as she loved Schubert Lieder, but to remind the survivors of her long struggle that there would be more in our futures than sorrow. In his light voice Fred was telling me not to waste another moment in grief, that it was time to get up and trip the light fantastic, that, like him, I could walk on air!

And just as Dietrich Fischer-Dieskau did, and as my mother taught me and all her students to remember, Astaire seemed to be talking to me personally as he sang to me to let go of despair before I got any older. Let go of the despair, little lady and dance! dance! dance!

So I did, tapping my foot gently against the floor while softly singing the tune along with Fred, tears wearing away at my face, as rhythm and melody, movement and feeling perfectly coalesced in his body's limber grace. I was exhausted by the events of the day, but I finally understood that, as spring would eventually come to Paris, not in a sudden radiance, but slowly, daily, a trickle of light here, a tiny ray of sun there, the grief which had held my face and voice in stone could be, would be, softened, first by tears, then by music and then by what I had thought for nearly two years was impossible, a sense of lightness and relief.

As I had wished for Mum to let go peacefully in those final days of her life back in Brisbane in a room that also glowed with a particular light, as I had encased myself in the dark solitude of Paris so that I could go through the experience of grieving without pushing it down or elevating it through either denial or prayer, I felt that she now was telling me, wishing for me, through the man dancing like a cloud, to let go too.

I knew I wouldn't be able to hold the light inside me, that stone might envelop me as the days and weeks, months and years went by. But I also knew that it would soften again, harden and then soften, like the ebb and flow of feelings in a day walking through Paris. Perhaps there is no one solution to grief, but like a change of season it transforms only incrementally, through a variety and range of consolations: the poetry that can understand its frozen depths, the song that can articulate and communicate it to another, the dance that can move it through you in a place which, by chance one day, can also make you part of a congregation of strangers looking, as mourners do, at light in the dark.

CONTRIBUTORS

Margaret Barbalet is a novelist, poet and former diplomat who was posted to Kuala Lumpur for three years in the mid-1990s and to Abu Dhabi from 2005 to 2008. She claims Katherine Mansfield, Bruce Dawe and Alice Munro as early influences. She now lives in Sydney and is working on her tenth book, a novel.

Nikki Barrowclough was born and grew up in New Zealand. She studied journalism in Auckland, has travelled widely and was a journalist at *The Sydney Morning Herald* and *Good Weekend* magazine from 1990 until 2012.

Caroline Baum is a journalist, broadcaster and producer. Born in the UK, she worked for Conde Nast, Time Life and the BBC before moving to Australia in 1984. Currently editorial director of Booktopia, Australia's largest online bookseller, she was the founding editor of *Good Reading* magazine and has been a contributor to the ABC, *The Sydney*

Morning Herald and national publications. www.carolinebaum.
com.au

Susan Duncan is the author of the memoirs *Salvation Creek*
and *The House at Salvation Creek*, *A Life on Pittwater* and a
work of fiction, *The Briny Cafe*, which is based on the water-
access-only area of Pittwater in NSW, where she lives with her
husband. Her new novel, *Gone Fishing*, is published in 2013.

Helen Garner was born in Geelong and lives in Melbourne.
Since 1977 she has published eleven books of fiction, essays
and long-form non-fiction, including *The First Stone* and
Joe Cinque's Consolation, as well as screenplays and feature
journalism. She won the inaugural Melbourne Prize for
Literature in 2006. Her most recent book is the novel *The
Spare Room*, which has been translated into many languages.

Kathryn Heyman is the author of *The Breaking* (shortlisted
for Scottish Writer of the Year Award, longlisted for the
Orange Prize), *Keep Your Hands on the Wheel* (Southern Arts
Award, adapted for BBC radio), *The Accomplice* (Arts Council
of England Writers Award, shortlisted for West Australian
Premier's Literary Awards) and *Captain Starlight's Apprentice*
(shortlisted for the Kibble Award, adapted for BBC radio).
Floodline, her fifth novel, was published in 2013.
www.kathrynheyman.com

Thomas Keneally is a Sydney writer, author of *The Chant of
Jimmy Blacksmith*, *Schindler's Ark*, *The Daughters of Mars* and a
series of histories named *Australians*. He has won the Booker
prize, the Mondello International Prize, the Helmerich

Award, and the Miles Franklin. A number of his books have been listed in *The New York Times* Books of the Year, and his study of famine, *Three Famines*, was a *Boston Globe* and *Los Angeles Times* Book of the Year.

David Marr is a journalist and author. He has written for Fairfax and broadcasts for the ABC. His books include lives of Patrick White and Garfield Barwick, and the most recent is *Political Animal: the Making of Tony Abbott*.

Linda Neil is a writer, musician and documentary producer whose work has won multiple international awards. Her family memoir, *Learning How to Breathe*, was long-listed for *The Age* Book of the Year non-fiction award in 2010, and in 2012 she was the Australia Council writer-in-residence at the Keesing Studio at the Internationale Cite des Arts in Paris.

Margaret Rice is a Sydney-based freelance journalist and writer with a special interest in medical and related social issues. She started her career at *The Sydney Morning Herald* and has worked at *The Australian* and as editor of the doctors' newspaper *Medical Observer*. She currently works as a sub-editor with Australian Associated Press and is writing a book inspired by the death of her mother.

Jaya Savige is Poetry Editor at *The Australian* newspaper. He is the author of *Latecomers* (UQP 2005), which won the NSW Premier's *Kenneth Slessor* Prize for Poetry, and *Surface to Air* (UQP 2011). He has recently completed a PhD as a Gates Scholar at the University of Cambridge, Christ's College, and is currently Lecturer in 19th–20th Century Literature at the New College of the Humanities, London.

Mandy Sayer is an award-winning novelist, memoirist and short story writer. Her most recent books are the novel *Love in the Years of Lunacy* and a volume of light humour, *Coco: Autobiography of My Dog.* She has also written about her parents extensively in the memoirs *Dreamtime Alice* and *Velocity.* Her third memoir will be published in 2014 by Allen & Unwin.

Gerard Windsor has published fiction, memoirs, essays, literary criticism and comic verse. He was awarded the 2005 Pascall Prize for Critical Writing. His most recent book is a non-fiction account of an Australian infantry company in Vietnam, *All Day Long the Noise of Battle.*

Susan Wyndham is the literary editor of *The Sydney Morning Herald.* In her career as a journalist she has been editor of *Good Weekend* magazine, New York correspondent for *The Australian* and a deputy editor of the *Herald.* She is the author of *Life In His Hands: The True Story of a Neurosurgeon and a Pianist,* and has edited and contributed to several other books.

ACKNOWLEDGEMENTS

THIS BOOK SPRANG TO LIFE AT the Allen & Unwin Christmas party in 2011, where I had an emotional conversation with publisher Jane Palfreyman about the deaths of her father and my mother during that year. She immediately shared my belief in the value of such a collection and helped turn it into a reality. I am most grateful for her enthusiastic support and her ideas, including the book's title, which is such an elegantly simple solution to a knotty challenge.

Thanks to Belinda Lee, senior editor at Allen & Unwin, and copyeditor Ali Lavau, who improved the book in so many ways with their sensitive, clear-eyed editing. And to Sandy Cull for a beautiful and eloquent cover. It was a pleasure to collaborate with some of the best professionals in publishing on the deeply satisfying process of making a book.

My greatest thanks go to the contributors, who responded to my request without hesitation and wrote about a private subject with generosity, originality and style. I am honoured to share these pages with them. On their behalf, I dedicate the book to our parents.

Susan Wyndham

Grateful acknowledgement is given for permission to reproduce extracts from the following works:

David Walsh, comments from the O device at the Museum of Old and New Art, Hobart, for the Anselm Kiefer work *Sternenfall/Shevirath ha Kelim*, 2007.

Anna Funder, *Stasiland*, published by The Text Publishing Company Australia © Anna Funder 2002.

Hilary Mantel, 'An experiment in love', used with the author's permission.

Jeff Duff 'In space everybody jams with Miles', lyrics used with his permission.

Dylan Thomas 'Do not go gentle into that good night', *Collected Poems: Dylan Thomas*, Orion, 2003.